THE POLITICS OF

HUMANISM

A CHRISTIAN RESPONSE TO THE
HUMANIST WORLDVIEW

THE POLITICS OF HUMANISM

A CHRISTIAN RESPONSE TO THE HUMANIST WORLDVIEW

JASON M. GARWOOD

CROSS & CROWN BOOKS
WARRENTON, VA

The Politics of Humanism
A Christian Response to the Humanist Worldview

Copyright 2020 © Jason M. Garwood

Publisher:
Cross & Crown Books
41 West Lee Highway
Suite 59 Box #199
Warrenton, VA 20186

Cover Design: Red Bag Media

Printed in the United States of America.

ISBN-13: 978-1-7341228-2-4

DEDICATION

To R.J. Rushdoony:

For seeing to it that we all know
how to push the *correct* antithesis.

CONTENTS

Acknowledgments

Foreword   1

1   Humanism: The Religion of Fallen Man   5

2   Socialism: The Politics of Fallen Man   19

3   Sexuality: The Sacraments of Fallen Man   33

4   Statist Education: The Discipleship of Fallen Man   47

5   Immigration: The Organization of Fallen Man   59

6   War: The Aggression of Fallen Man   77

7   Drug War: The Slavery of Fallen Man   93

8   Gun Control: The Statist Protections of Fallen Man   107

9   Racism: The Prejudice of Fallen Man   121

10   Kingdom: The Vision of Redeemed Man   139

Epilogue   151

Appendix 1: Vaccines: The Gospel Imperative to End the Silence   153

About the Author

ACKNOWLEDGMENTS

Thank you, Jesus, for being enthroned and guiding every detail of my life. Thank you, Jordan, for helping me get the page numbers formatted after several frustrating attempts. (The curse is real!) *Many* thanks to my brother, Brett, and Red Bag Media for the cover design!

I also want to thank my wife, Mary, for being my best friend; my children for bringing me joy; and the day-to-day blessing that is my Cross & Crown family.

FOREWORD

THE BOOK YOU ARE HOLDING IN YOUR hands started out as a sermon series I preached in our fellowship in 2018. For a long time, I have wanted to address these issues because they are either largely ignored by Christians or (sadly) never preached about in the pulpit. It is not as though God's Word has nothing to say about the topics in question—otherwise we can pack up and go home. The problem is that the Bible says a whole *lot* about these things and most preachers do not care to do the hard work of exegesis and application. It is not difficult to see where the Bible deals with things like the drug war, racism, and education. The problem comes in when you have to stand up in front of the people who pay your salary and unashamedly proclaim, "Thus saith the Lord."

It is remarkably easy to pound the podium and declare that justification is on the basis of faith alone, and not works, or that the gospel is "Jesus died for your sins." The milk of the word, although essential for laying a sturdy foundation, tends be treated as though it's the *height* of Christian experience. Preachers dole out the milk bottles while their congregations suckle on the teat of ease and convenience.

Due to the institution's obligation to pay the staff and mortgage, and grow the business model (churches are really good at free market competition, especially when it comes to Easter egg helicopter drops), the goal can *never* be discipleship and the faith for all of life, for this is a rival program that runs contrary to their business needs and goals.

There's a direct correlation between the pietistic preaching of milk and the centrality of the church as an institution. When the institution serves as the main hub for the Christian life (instead of the Kingdom), the only thing the preacher can do is ensure that his listeners feel guilty about serving Christ *outside* the walls of a local church. To do this, he must not get into 'worldly' issues that do not have anything to do with his institutionalism (what does Christianity have to do with public schools?). He must distract them with bread and circuses, handwringing, and nervousness about the future. Silence becomes his best friend.

If he were to speak out on things like the drug war, racism, or the abhorrent government education system, he might endanger his career by turning people loose from the institution in order the combat these sins and idols. If this happens, his career will be found to be in jeopardy and his institutional programs will crumble. The brand? It will fail. The marketing and mailers? No one will bother. His job? Pointless: everyone has surpassed him. This is why the modern Church is at odds with kingdom of God. The kingdom of God has been and will always be a threat and a rival to the kingdoms of men—including, but not limited to, the *ecclesiastical* kingdoms of men.

I could go on and on listing example after example of all the ways we've misunderstood the Great Commission and the gospel of the *Kingdom*. But that's for another book at another time.

The Politics of Humanism is a journey through the various ways in which humanism is at odds with the politics of Jesus. The hope is that you, the reader, will be challenged to further explore the antithesis between the kingdom of God and the sham that is kingdoms of men. Most importantly, however, is the hope that you will find the Scriptures to be refreshingly authoritative on the issues we face today. We are in dire need of right *thinking* and right *doing*. So, *tolle lege*, and maybe we can reconstruct some things in the process.

Jason Garwood
Warrenton, VA
February 11, 2020

ONE

HUMANISM: THE RELIGION OF FALLEN MAN

Not to us, O Lord, not to us, but to your name give glory,
for the sake of your steadfast love and your faithfulness. Why should
the nations say, "Where is their God?" Our God is in the heavens; he
does whatever he pleases. Their idols are silver and gold, the work of
human hands. They have mouths, but do not speak; eyes, but do not
see. They have ears, but do not hear; noses, but do not smell. They
have hands, but do not feel; feet, but do not walk; they make no sound
in their throats. Those who make them are like them; so are all who
trust in them. O Israel, trust in the Lord! He is their help and their
shield.

Psalm 115:1-9

THE DOCTRINE OF HUMANISM IS BOTH A
growing trend and a growing problem. This means that
if we want to be faithful Christians in an age of rampant,
unbridled humanism, we must know our interlocutors
and be able to dismantle their ungodly worldview. If it
is true that our job is to take the land and Christianize it,
and that is absolutely what the Great Commission is all

about, then it follows from this that we must be committed to understanding the rival, anti-Christian worldviews that are being pontificated in the public square. When we *understand* them, we can thus *dismantle* them—and dismantle we *must* do. That's the logic behind why I wrote this book. That and because the Church has by and large refused to discuss any of these topics for various reasons we will get into.

As the reader will see shortly, humanism can be a tricky thing to nail to the wall because like *Jello-O*, it's squirmy when you touch it. This means that I am going to spend a lot of time referencing various people and various works so you get an idea of what it is that's being said, and, hopefully, when we look at various texts from Scripture, we will be better prepared and equipped to bring forth the onslaught of our apologetic.

In this chapter we are going to examine humanism in general and show from the Bible why humanism is the religion of fallen man. Humanists would already be frustrated because they do not see themselves as being religious, but the reality is, they are the most ardent of religious people. Men in their sins will default to a humanist religion long before bowing the knee to their Creator. Apart from grace, that is where we *all* begin.

In the following pages we will pull apart the various layers of this religious dogma by looking at the philosophical underpinnings of the worldview, and how those philosophies work themselves out into every area of life. Humanism is a religion of dominion, make no mistake, and the folly does seep into every area of life. As such, we will cover things like socialism, sexuality, education, immigration, just war, the drug war, guns, and racism. Everywhere you look, humanism is attempting to be the religious and social order of the day, so we must not be silent about it. Having said all that, let's get to work.

It was Monday, October 29, 1945 when the 40-year-old French philosopher Jean-Paul Sartre delivered a lecture at Club Maintenant in Paris called, "Existentialism is a humanism." Two years before this, Sartre had published *Being and Nothingness*, and since that had caused quite a stir, he accepted the invitation to lecture on existentialism with the hope of correcting his detractors. On the one hand, the Catholics and Christians criticized his views; on the other hand, the Communists were offering their fair share of disdain. In light of this brush fire, Sartre needed to clear the air and did so that Monday evening in Paris.

Most certainly not the first existentialist (Kierkegaard is largely considered to be its founder, though he never used the term), Sartre delivered his understanding of humanist philosophy through the lens of existentialism. While he somewhat disagreed with Kierkegaard the Danish philosopher, Dostoevsky the

7

Russian novelist and philosopher, and Nietzsche the German philosopher, these men shared something in common despite living in different times: *man is the starting point for all discussion and philosophy.* With the Enlightenment's emphasis on rationalism, skepticism, and a rejection of God, this man-centered insistence helped launch the existentialist movement, with thanksgiving and praise heaped onto men like René Descartes, John Locke, and David Hume. With God out of the way and declared dead, man could only look to himself (how convenient). This is where Sartre comes in.

Sartre's famous quip 'existence precedes essence' formed the thrust of his existentialistic humanism. What he argued was that man *begins* with existence—without any foreordination or preset expectations—and *then* follows this existence with his essence, his personality.

In other words, to quote Sartre on what he means by this:

> Man first exists: he materializes in the world, encounters himself, and only afterward defines himself. If man, as existentialists conceive of him, cannot be defined it is because to begin with he is nothing. He will not be anything until later, and then he will be what he makes of himself. Thus, there is no human nature since there is no God to conceive of it. Man is not only that which he conceives himself to be, but that which he wills himself to be, and since he conceives of himself only after he exists, just as he wills himself to be after being thrown into

8

existence, man is nothing other than what he makes himself. This is the first principle of existentialism.[1]

Hopefully you caught the nonsense here. He presupposes that God does not exist, and with this presupposition comes attached to it *zero expectation of meaning.* Man is brought into the world, no strings attached. No moral, philosophical expectations are involved; then, and only then, can he begin to define himself and the world around him. Sartre also says that man is not just what he can dream up, it's what he wills for himself, what he *does.* In Sartre's worldview, man has the privilege of writing the dictionary and making his own reality.

Since humanists like Sartre and others cannot and will not submit themselves to God, they are forced to create a system of explaining the world that is both free from external consequence, and free from having to submit to God's desires. After all, it was Dostoevsky who once remarked, "If God does not exist, everything is permissible."

I hope you can see the destructive nature of humanism, and I want to now look at our text here in Psalm 115 to demonstrate further the folly of the humanist religion.

In verse one the psalmist gives us the

---

[1] Jean-Paul Sartre, *Existentialism Is a Humanism*, (New Haven, CT: Yale University Press, 2007), 22.

presuppositional starting point:

> Not to us, O Lord, not to us, but to your name give glory,
> for the sake of your steadfast love and your faithfulness.

God gets the glory, not man. We start with God the Creator and his lovingkindness and truth. The context here is with regard to Israel being mocked for its weakness, its helplessness. They were being chided for their trust and hope in the Lord. For the humanist mocker who says in verse two, "Where is their God?" we must understand that the only god that is acceptable to them is a god who serves *their* desires, who meets *their* demands, who acquiesces to *their* requirements.

Essentially the writer begins by saying, *God, the glory is yours, not ours, so why would you allow our enemies to taunt you? To question you and demean you?* The opening plea is for God to step in and not allow the scoffing to continue unchallenged.

Now, at this point, we could stop reading and assume that the writer (and we who think the same things) should go about whining of our condition and retreating from the world. Indeed this is what the Church today has largely done. Instead of building and fighting, she has retreated and bellyached. But the writer does no such thing, and nor should we. What does the psalmist suggest next? *The idols of the heathens are impotent and obtuse.* Our God is in the heavens, which means he is the true sovereign and he does whatever pleases his sovereign will (v. 3). What about the gods of the heathens? Verse four says that they are silver and gold, which means they pulled them out of God's earth and fashioned them with the hands God gave them. So much for autonomy.

> They have mouths, but do not speak; eyes, but do not see.
> They have ears, but do not hear; noses, but do not smell.
> They have hands, but do not feel; feet, but do not walk;
> they make no sound in their throats. (vv. 5-7)

They are completely and entirely impotent and inconsequential. For the humanist religion, the purpose of their god is to serve their declared word. But the Biblical religion, the faith of the one true God, is a faith that serves the God of Creation. God is not to be counseled or governed by man, rather, man is counseled and governed by God.

It is interesting the way in which the Bible describes the false gods: they cannot speak, cannot see, cannot hear, and cannot smell. They cannot feel, cannot walk and cannot even make so much as a peep with their throat. Interestingly, animals *can* do these things; but false gods cannot. Idols are lifeless, meaningless, purposeless, and ultimately powerless. They are beneath even the animals.

Look at verse eight:

> Those who make them are like them; so are all who trust in them.

The end goal of people who worship false gods—and I am purposefully throwing all the false religions of the world into the same humanist basket—is that *they become like the gods they worship.* Be it the naturalist, nihilist, Mormon, or Muslim, all of them become like that which they worship: radically *impotent,* and arrogantly *incompetent.* Ultimately these idols and the people that follow them will be frustrated and powerless in history. Their impotence is clearly seen in the fact that their man-centered religion is the root problem, and thus in their futility, they think they can fix it themselves. Man is the problem, that we agree. However, the answer is not found in man; but the humanist thinks he can find it there.

In prepping for this chapter, I decided to go online to see what modern-day humanists are saying. To start, I found the *International Humanist and Ethical Union* website, and here is their definition of humanism:

> Humanism is a democratic and ethical life stance that affirms that human beings have the right and responsibility to give meaning and shape to their own lives. Humanism stands for the building of a more humane society through an ethics based on human and other natural values in a spirit of reason and free inquiry through human capabilities. Humanism is not theistic, and it does not accept supernatural views of reality.[2]

---

[2] https://humanists.international/what-is-humanism (accessed January 3, 2020).

Take note the viciously circular problem here: Humans must give shape to their own lives (notice the influence of Sartre's thinking), and thus they are free to do as they please. However, they know that can sound crazy because pedophiles do as *they* please. Anticipating this objection, they need to establish an ethical grid so they can create their own little version of a 'more humane society' and they base that on "human and other natural values in a spirit of reason and free inquiry through human capabilities." They aren't saying anything substantive, by the way. In their minds, humans should shape their own destiny with no outside control (read 'no God') and in order to do that in their pursuit of this meaning and shaping they must be somewhat ethically reasonable, *but that is sort of a natural thing that comes about anyway.* Right. It's nonsensical rubbish, really.

Another website is *Humanists UK*, a place dedicated to the humanist religion in the United Kingdom. The heading of one section reads, "Think for yourself, act for everyone."[3] This was followed up with another statement:

> At Humanists UK, we want a tolerant world where rational thinking and kindness prevail. We work to support lasting change for a better society, championing ideas for the one life we have. We do this because we're humanists, people who shape our own lives in the here and now, because we

[3] https://humanism.org.uk (accessed January 3, 2020).

believe it's the only life we get.

One book I read is called *Humanism* by Stephen Law. [4] Mr. Law is "Reader in Philosophy" at Heythrop College, University of London, and is editor of the Royal Institute of Philosophy journal called THINK. In his little book he describes in a nutshell what humanists believe:

1. Humanists believe since, and reason more generally, are invaluable tools we can and should apply to all areas of life. No beliefs should be considered off-limits and protected from rational scrutiny.

2. Humanists are either atheists or at least agnostic.

3. Humanists believe that this life is the only life we have.

4. Humanisms involves a commitment to the existence and importance of moral value. Ethics should be strongly informed by study of what human beings are actually like, and of what will help them flourish in this world, rather than the next.

5. Humanists emphasize individual moral autonomy. They reject external authority hanging over one's head telling them what is right and wrong.

6. Humanists believe our lives can have meaning without it being bestowed from above by God.

7. Humanists are secularists, in the sense that they favor an open, democratic society in which the state takes a neutral position with respect to religion.

As you can see, humanism is a deeply problematic

---

[4] Stephen Law, *Humanism: A Very Short Introduction*, (New York, NY: Oxford University Press, 2011).

worldview with inconsistencies running all the way through, and this is because the answer to the question, "What is man?" is answered with, "Whatever he wants to be."

This is a question we absolutely *should* be asking. The problem, though, is the humanist can only conceive of an answer in terms of himself. He cannot look past himself into the realm of the metaphysical, the truly transcendent, the sovereign. *This is because he will not submit to an external word, an external authority.*

At the root level, humanism is self-refuting and self-blinding. Humanists refuse to look beyond themselves to the one true God. When he throws off his obligation to serve God, his pursuit becomes a 'disintegration into the void', as Cornelius Van Til has taught us. His quest becomes a pursuit of blindness, speechlessness, and idiocy. When man looks to himself for the answers, he goes further and further into sin and darkness. He is dull, and he is dead. No matter what these humanist scholars say—and they *sound* smart—they see themselves as the word of truth, the source of revelation, and the source of power. They are putting forth a rival religion and rival social order, one where the philosopher-kings rule and reign.

The problem here is that his religion is unable to reform and revive himself. His religion only serves to execute his lusts as he burns with desire. This is the same problem that traces all the way back to Genesis 3:5, when Adam and Eve wanted to become a law unto themselves. They wanted to determine good and evil on their terms. This humanistic spirit has rippled through the halls of history and time, and the logical outcome of this greedy pursuit is destruction and ruin.

You see, the gospel restores a man to his dominion calling under God. Without this restoration man is dead in his humanist religion and unable to have dominion the way God intends. However, he still *tries* to have dominion—a perverted dominion, nonetheless. Notice that both Stephen Law and the one website both spoke in terms of 'all of life'. The Church at large won't speak in those terms, but you better believe that the humanists are doing so. Without the gospel of Jesus Christ restoring a man to his calling under God, he cannot and will not submit to God, and thus he will seek to dominate other men. It's the difference between the (biblical) dominion religion and the (satanic) power religion.

This 'do-it-yourself' religion, as Rushdoony has called it, is a man-made morality and ethical outlook that seeks to legislate sin and perpetuate immorality. There is a reason why after the Enlightenment, and during the 19th and 20th centuries, we had a rise in revolutionary activity. The humanistic religion took politics by storm with the rise of Marxism and Communism. The state became god and man became the means of upholding this god. Millions and millions of lives were snuffed out all in the name of humanism and the 'Great Leap Forward'. These totalitarian politics ushered in the new age of man, one where the state controls every area of life and thus helps dictate that which *is* and that which *will be*. It was and is entirely destructive because their gods are foolish and incompetent, carelessly throwing themselves about without consideration of what is left in their wake. It's an unholy postmillennialism.

So, Christian, what must we do? We must understand the *politics* of humanism by understanding humanism as a philosophical worldview. We must see how pervasive this thinking is—both in public schools and at the university. We must know how to do true presuppositionalism and how to apply the entirety of the Bible to all of life. We must be bold and courageous enough to speak to the issues and offer up a truly biblical answer. We must know biblical law. We must take seriously the gospel of the Kingdom of God. It's *our* problem, and we must deal with it.

TWO

SOCIALISM: THE POLITICS OF FALLEN MAN

You shall not steal.

Exodus 20:15

WHEN IT COMES TO HUMANISM, WHICH, AS we saw in the last chapter, is the *religion* of fallen man, we need to keep in mind that this religion of fallen man also has a political component as well. Not only is the humanist a person with *religious* convictions, he is also a person with *political* convictions as well. Since his religious convictions will always lead him to develop a system of man-centered political contrivances, it follows quite naturally and logically that the humanist will pursue socialism as his political order. The reason for this is because in his arrogance, the humanist has declared God to be dead, revolting against God and God's sovereignty. As a result, he must assert that he himself is alive and well and is the ultimate presupposition, thus removing God and asserting himself as the sovereign.

Sovereignty presupposes jurisdiction, and jurisdiction requires a law order.

However, the challenge for the humanist is this: in order for him to structure the world, he must develop a coherent social order that coincides with his religious presuppositions. Considering the fact that he hates God and will not submit to him, he is now forced to relinquish and renounce individual liberty because only the transcendent and Triune God of heaven grants a man individual liberty. Man cannot grant another man liberty. He can only rule over him or serve him. Civil government does not grant freedom; it can only chip away at freedom and take it away altogether.

The only way to answer the dialectical problem of the One and the Many—individual liberty verses the collective of all mankind—the humanist has to follow the Hegelian model which eliminates one of those, and thus he favors the collective over against the individual.[5] [As a side note, it was Cornelius Van Til who taught that 'all non-biblical thought is inherently dialectical,' and consequently, Christianity is the only possible way to solve the dilemma of the One and the Many, and this is solved because the ultimately One and Many is the Triune Godhead.]

At any rate, because man in his sin rejects the

---

[5] See my article, https://www.lambsreign.com/blog/dialectical-ninnyhammers

transcendency of God, he must develop his system from his own self-generated religious convictions. Consequently, he chooses the collective as taking primacy over of the individual and this is because he hates the liberty that God's law grants him. I did not say something wrong here: *the humanist hates the liberty that God's law grants to him.* Rejecting God's law leads to tyranny, not freedom. Its rejection does not liberate a man, it enslaves him. Tyranny exist because men would much rather have someone else do the governing than do the hard work and discipline of self-governance. More on that later.

Now, when we talk about socialism, we would be remiss to leave out of the picture the most influential man behind the socialist vision, and that being Communism's chief thinker, Karl Marx.

Karl 'What's mine is mine and what's yours is mine' Marx was a constantly quarreling, wild donkey of a man. He spent his nights drinking and talking and often spent his days sleeping on the couch in the clothes he wore the previous day. Marx, whose anger was a tremendous problem, would often say to the people he didn't like, "I will annihilate you."[6]

---

[6] I recommend you pick up: Paul Johnson, *Intellectuals* (New York, NY: Harper Perennial, 2007). His biographical sketch of Marx is incredibly helpful and much of what I have written here has been influenced by him. I also suggest reading Dr. Gary North's book, *Marx's Religion of Revolution*, and that can be found online for free:

Which is interesting coming from a man whose health was always a problem, who was without personal hygiene, and whose self-control was so lacking that he squandered the money he borrowed from friends and family. Once he pursued a job, and really only once. He was a burly, surly curmudgeon whose ideas, once they got out there, most certainly led to the mass murder of nearly 100 million people through the vehicle of Communism.

In 1848, he, along with his friend Fredrich Engels, published *The Communist Manifesto*, and in it they painted their eschatological vision for the destruction of capitalism and anything remotely close to the Christian faith. This piece of literature has influenced more people than any other piece of literature in history—second only to the Bible. Marx's philosophy was simple: "Socialism cannot be brought into existence without revolution." And revolution was indeed the vision of a man whose demons poisoned him to the point of usurping anything close to individual liberty. This, too, is ironic given the life of Marx.

His book *Capital* was a self-deceived concoction consisting of plagiarism, outdated information, and a refusal to see or state the facts. One example will suffice. Marx wrote a chapter essentially critiquing the working conditions of men in the capitalistic factories during the

Industrial Revolution in England. *He never once stepped foot in a factory.* In fact, much of the information he used was outdated five, ten, and even twenty years from the time of his writing. Capitalism most certainly self-corrected those problems (as the free market always does), but Marx conveniently ignored the facts in order to push his demonic agenda.

Speaking of Marx's complete and utter hypocrisy, his own mother poked a hole in his entire philosophy when she wished that "Karl would accumulate capital instead of just writing about it." It is well known and established that Marx's personality was devoid and defunct of integrity. So how does someone like him impact so many around the world? The answer has several layers, but we will start with the simple concept of *vision.*

Despite the trouble outlined previously, we know that the man whose liver always gave him trouble could still *see.* He was a distressed revolutionary whose anger, strife, and lack of self-control fueled a fire for inexorable covetousness and greed. Only when a person completely bereft of integrity and self-government under God can he come up with an eschatological vision of mass destruction. And *yes,* it was a vision of mass destruction. Do not be deceived: Marx had a vision for the future, which cannot be said of the modern Church.

On one level, sin and rebellion are the seeds of

humanism. This goes all the way back to the sin of Adam and Eve in the garden when they wanted to know and determine good and evil for themselves (Gen. 3:5). On another level, this isn't *merely* a metaphysical thing. Those seeds, planted in the anti-Semitic heart of Marx, sprouted forth into a comprehensive, all-of-life vision for society—and thus it produced the politics of fallen man, what we call socialism. Before we unpack this dangerous doctrine some more, let's look at the text before us.

Exodus 20:15 reads, "You shall not steal." The word 'steal' means 'to take by stealth,' or 'to take or remove something secretly without the knowledge of the person who possesses it'. Implicit within this command is the notion of private property. For someone to 'steal' something means the forced removal a possession from someone else, and it logically follows, then, that the thing possessed had its rightful owner. What we call the 'negativism' of the law is clear: do not steal. Do *not* do *this*. However, as is the case in biblical law, there is a positivism to it: acknowledge and respect private property; generate wealth and support others voluntarily in this process. We might even say that inferred within this law is the notion of freely giving to those in need.

The Bible lays out a vision for private property when it says things like, "The earth is the Lord's and all that is in it, the world, and those who live in it;" (Psalm

24:1). Also found in the Bible is Psalm 50:10-12, which reads:

> For every wild animal of the forest is mine, the cattle on a thousand hills. I know all the birds of the air, and all that moves in the field is mine. If I were hungry, I would not tell you, for the world and all that is in it is mine.

What is explicit throughout the entirety of the Bible is the fact that *God grants dominion to man, but he does not grant ultimate sovereignty.* The ultimate owner and landlord of all property on earth is God who created all of it. This exercise of *ultimate* sovereignty is not delegated to man. In short: *Man is given private property and jurisdiction over material things from the hand of God who owns it all.* This is a derivative sovereignty, what we might call a sovereignty of material stewardship under God. The earth is the Lord's, this is true. But it is also given to man to steward and subdue, to work and keep and build the kingdom of God on earth as it is in heaven. Christian theology, labor, and work is tied to man's responsibility before God. We do not work as a punishment for our sin, we work because this was God's intention all along, to fill the earth and subdue it; to make it fruitful and productive.

All of which is to say, private property is a doctrine that is derived from the Bible and from the mind of God. It is a real concept, and any time anyone gets this right, it is because of the Christian worldview which grants coherence to these ideas. Theft, which is a sin and a violation of God's law-order, is not just a transaction between men, it's a sin against God. God demands that we treat one another with respect and dignity, and this is accomplished in all of our relationships when we *don't steal things from each other.*

Listen, there is never going to be a justifiable doctrine and political philosophy that can possibly overturn the eighth commandment *regardless* of what man says. We cannot rationalize our way into violating this commandment, saying things like, 'Well I needed this particular thing more than he did'. Nor can we justify the violation of this commandment by saying things like, 'Well, if the state does it, it's OK'.

God's sovereignty and the administration of his law-word demands that his law take precedent and priority over everything else. The only legitimate way to obtain wealth is through work, inheritance, or gift. *That's it.* We are called to work via the dominion mandate, and we cannot circumvent this calling by stealing from others. This is where socialism comes in.

It is no secret that the first of the ten planks of the Communist Manifesto reads, "Abolition of private property in land and application of all rents of land to public purpose." In order for Marx to achieve his eschatological vision for a dictatorship at the hands of the proletariat, he had to get rid of the most foundational element of a free society under God: private property.

Once Marx could seize land, he could then carry out the rest of his agenda: a heavy, progressive or graduated income tax; abolition of all rights of inheritance; confiscation of the property of all emigrants and rebels; centralization of credit in the hands of the state by means of a national bank with state capital and an exclusive monopoly; centralization of the means of communication and transportation in the hands of the state; grow the state's ownership of factories and means of production; equal obligation of all to work and the establishment of industrial armies, especially for agriculture; combine agriculture and manufacturing industries, and get rid of the distinction between town and country and distribute people evenly; free education in government schools.

If you read all of that without me telling you it was Marx and Engel's *Communist Manifesto*, you would probably think I was talking about America. Well, the truth is, America *is* a socialist country, and America doesn't seem to care, Christians included.

According to Friedrich Hayek, "Socialism means the abolition of private enterprise, of private ownership of the means of production, and the creation of a system of 'planned economy' in which the entrepreneur working for profit is replaced by a central planning body."[7]

Socialism itself began with a much simpler definition, and that being "government ownership of the means of production." But as Hayek carefully nuances, this definition evolved a bit in the twentieth century and now it means the redistribution of income in pursuit of equality, not through government ownership of labor and means of production *per se*, but through institutions of the welfare state and progressive income tax. In other words, the goal has always been this elusive 'equality', but the means have shifted a bit. As Orwell put it in *Animal Farm*, "All animals are equal, but some animals are more equal than others." It is ironic that the socialist vision for equality is anything but equality, especially when it comes to the progressive income tax: the rich are taxed more, and thus they are not equal under law. America has tinkered with the socialist practice of income tax since 1913.

Socialism is the political choice of fallen man because socialism is the answer to man's quest for a social order built on his religious presuppositions. In other words, humanism as a *philosophy* doesn't do anything to build a social order. There's no tangible vision in ethereal concepts, no practical day-to-day dealings with economics and law and order. For the humanist to make

---

[7] Friedrich Hayek, *Road to Serfdom, Volume II* (New York, NY: Routledge, 2014), 83.

his vision for society come to fruition, he has to look to socialism and here's why.

I mentioned briefly a bit ago the problem of the One and the Many. In philosophy, there is always a dialectical tension between the individual and the collective. Which matters more: the individual or the group? The one person or everyone together? As Christians who understand that God has revealed himself to us in Christ and through His Word, we know that we're the only ones who can solve this dilemma. But that doesn't mean that the humanist won't try. The problem of the One and the Many is not solved by eliminating one in favor of the other. Statism, and thus socialism, erroneously overemphasizes the collective at the expense of the individual. The whole socialist scheme centralizes everything, bringing it into One. *Everything* is done via central planning. The elite group at the top, who are more equal than others, dictate to the rest at the bottom what the central planning goals are to be. They are the rulers, and we're told that we must trust them.

The humanist must do this in order to carry out his vision for the future. Marx had to cut to the foundation of property rights granted from God in order to see a revolution. *All material things come from God's hand.* Thus, everything that is given to us, or earned by us, is from his gracious storehouses. *If we begin here, we can start with the abolition of this very concept of God's ownership and our derivative ownership, and then we can get on with imposing our collectivist vision.* People are induced to steal the goods and possessions of others because they do not trust God, and therefore pollute themselves with greed and covetousness. Marx hated capitalism, and anything related to it, especially the Jews. So, what must he do? *He must take from them.* In his lust, he must take from them and break the eighth commandment in the process. This is the core of the socialist agenda: *theft.*

The socialist mantra, "The greatest good for the greatest number of people" is nothing more than smoke and mirrors sloganeering. Whether it's the fascism of Benito Mussolini in Italy, the communism of Stalin in Soviet Russia, or the German fascism which arrived in full swing with Hitler himself, the common denominator in all of it is this: *Individuals can and should be sacrificed for the greater good of the collective.* The solution for Marx and others like him was to simply remove the individual from the equation. You are not human, you have no rights. [This is why Jews in the ghettos and concentration camps were given numbers instead of names.]

Here's the thing…

Man was created to be free. But this freedom, this liberty, could only be exercised and ascertained by man in subordination to God. The only true freedom and

30

liberty a man can possess is that which is in service and obedience to God. Because of this, paganism will always need statism (the collective), through the means of socialism, in order to control and manage the individual. Pagan man can never be free because pagan man will only submit to a self-created godhead and self-created social order. All unbiblical thinking will result in the collective taking precedence over the individual. *Always*. This is why Hillary Clinton can speak of all the children as being property of the state. All socialists say these things because that's part of the scheme. Republicans and other ostensible conservatives are no different when they speak of 'our public schools'.

In response, what we must do as Christians at every turn is insist on individual liberty. And I'll tell you this much, it's going to be very hard to do because socialism has run through just about everything in our country, from public schools and excessive taxation, to inheritance taxes and price controls, socialism is here and it will not go away without the Christian vision for a coherent social order based on God's law and God's prescription for individual liberty.

Socialism is a dangerous doctrine forged from the political and religious fires of God-denying humanism. Socialism destroys entrepreneurial ingenuity, technological advancement, and economic improvement because it robs a man of the incentive to fulfill the dominion calling God has placed upon him. Everything socialism has touched it has destroyed. There are no redeeming qualities, and thus it is completely and entirely incompatible with the Christian faith.

Entrepreneurship and technological advancement can only come from the hands of a man who not only believes himself to be free but is truly and objectively free to explore the world that God has created. You do not get the iPhone from a tyrannical, totalitarian regime who wants to control and dictate not only the *labor* of a man, but the *vision* of a man.

So, we must fight against it. We must not participate in the socialistic schemes of modern America. We must refrain from taking the government's cheese and 'free' education. We must be diligent in getting this message to the masses, starting locally and starting today. There is so much work to be done to combat this ginormous problem, and we have no time to waste. We must pray, and we must fight. And we must not see this as secondary: this is primary because *the gospel of the Kingdom of God is entirely opposed to socialism.*

THREE

SEXUALITY: THE SACRAMENTS OF FALLEN MAN

For this reason God gave them up to degrading passions. Their women exchanged natural intercourse for unnatural, and in the same way also the men, giving up natural intercourse with women, were consumed with passion for one another. Men committed shameless acts with men and received in their own persons the due penalty for their error. And since they did not see fit to acknowledge God, God gave them up to a debased mind and to things that should not be done. They were filled with every kind of wickedness, evil, covetousness, malice. Full of envy, murder, strife, deceit, craftiness, they are gossips, slanderers, God-haters, insolent, haughty, boastful, inventors of evil, rebellious toward parents, foolish, faithless, heartless, ruthless. They know God's decree, that those who practice such things deserve to die—yet they not only do them but even applaud others who practice them.

Romans 1:26-32

WITHOUT A DOUBT THE HUMANIST VISION is a comprehensive faith for all of life. Whether we're talking about Sartre's claim that man first exists and then shapes his own reality, or Marx's vision of dialectical materialism, these men, and others like them, believed in a full-orbed, faith for *all* of life. As Protagoras had said

33

way back in the fifth century B.C., "Man is the measure of all things." Due to the fact that the humanist always starts with man, and because he believes that man is truly the standard through which we view everything else, he is forced to provide answers for life solely in terms of himself. When Plato came along and interpreted what Protagoras had said, he took it to mean that there is no such thing as absolute truth, and that truth is what you make it. Sound familiar?

What's clear in our day is that Western civilization is undergoing a social revolution on a colossal scale. This revolution has innumerable layers to it (its origins are wide and varied), but at the core is a revolution of law and order, and this is because the religious convictions of Westerners have changed. As Rushdoony has taught us, any change in society will have an outward change in law, and underneath that is a change of religious conviction. The gods of the ancient past are obstreperously resurfacing, and this is due to the fact that paganism/humanism is now the new religion of the West.

Paganism, while usually used as a short-hand way of describing a 'heathen', actually comes from something quite different. The Latin word *paganus* means 'country dweller', or a villager in the countryside. In its original meaning, it was used to denote someone who lived in a rural setting, but it also meant someone who believed in folklore in the rural setting. The meaning, then, came to denote someone who worships the earth, or the self, as divine. Dr. Peter Jones calls this 'Oneism', meaning that there is no distinction between the Creator and creation, per Romans 1—which we just saw at the start of this chapter. Instead of the 'Twoism' of biblical Christianity, which sees a *difference* between the Creator and the created order, paganism rejects this binary existence and prefers to collapse everything into *One*.

When I say that the West has now adopted the religion of paganism, I'm simply saying that the Christian worldview has been rejected and replaced by a view of the world centered completely on man and the material. As we saw in the last chapter with Karl Marx, materialism, or what is sometimes called *naturalism*, sees man as simply being matter in motion and as a result, the only thing we have is what is tangibly before us. We are inexplicably living here on a rock floating in space and the only thing that matters is that nothing matters because your job is to make your own existence and worship everything material as divine because divinity is within us. This is the spirit of paganism.

As has been customary of this book thus far, I have tried to highlight certain intellectual personalities behind much of the humanist movement and this chapter will be no different.

Regarding the New Age movement and paganism,

Carl Jung is considered to be its founder. The Swiss psychiatrist was born on July 26, 1875 and is the person who coined the terms 'extrovert' and 'introvert'. If you've ever used the Myers-Briggs personality type system, you are no doubt using Jung's theories.

Jung saw himself as the mastermind and architect of 'a new humanism'. He lived during an exciting time as much work was being done in the field of psychoanalysis. While heavily influenced by Indian spirituality, Jung's psychologizing of religion spilled over into philosophy, anthropology, and even archaeology as well. His world renown drew the attention of Sigmund Freud who was 19 years older than Jung.

The work of Freud and Jung brought to the Western world a new field of discipline, one which gave scientific analysis of human behavior, thereby providing alleged answers to mankind's troubles. These two giants were not without differences of opinion, however. Jung preferred using psychology in conjunction with spirituality, while Freud was adamantly against religion, believing it to be nothing more than the illusions of desperate people. Jung's messianic complex (not an exaggeration) led him down the path of paranormal phenomena, most assuredly leading him to demonic experiences.

Carl Jung's father was a Lutheran minister, so he was exposed to Christianity at a young age. (We might be better to state that Carl was exposed to a *terrible* version of Christianity). His maternal grandparents were occultists, and one author documents the fact that Carl's mother was a medium who spent long periods "enthralled by the spirits that visited her at night."[8] Jung attended séances with his mother and no doubt dabbled in this form of necromancy several times over. This eventually led Jung to reject Jesus who "never became quite real for me," and thus he started his downward spiral into paganism.

For Jung, the only way to heal one's self is by realizing that divinity is inherently lodged inside all of us. Pagan myth must be brought into a man's mind and conscience. And this is where all of this is going, especially when we talk about human sexuality. The key for the humanist vision in the mind of Jung is *the elimination of all opposites.* When you relativize good and evil, collapsing them into a mere figment of one's imagination, you can then journey on towards the inward healing of self. Any inner contradictions, discomforts, or troubled ideas can be eliminated, and when you rid the world of its binary existence, it's only natural, then, that male and female become one. In fact, Christopher Roman, who would later become a transgender model named Carmen Carrera, said, "I am

---

[8] See Peter Jones, *The Other Worldview: Exposing Christianity's Greatest Threat* (Bellingham, WA: Kirkdale Press, 2015).

Adam. I am Eve. I am me." We'll cover more about androgyny later.

Jung's psychoanalysis was fueled by pagan spirituality, and because of the presuppositions attached to it, inevitably led him to believe that society could transcend 'type and sex'. Without a doubt, Jung's work contributed to the sexual revolution of the 1960's, even though he died in 1961 and could not see the terrible fruit of his paganism. Some see him as the first Christian counselor, which is altogether problematic, while atheistic humanists dismiss him, citing that he is far too religious for them.

What is clear, however, is that for Carl Jung, 'Nothing matters but the completion of self'. This is the same language we hear on television from Dr. Phil and Oprah. When an individual throws off the demands of the holy God, he can now fulfill his personal desires through science-based psychological maturity and sanctification. When we reach 'individuation', which is the process of maturing our subconscious, we are then liberated and transformed, so they say.

In Romans 1, the Apostle Paul paints the picture of fallen man and what fallen man does apart from God. At the core is his exchange of the truth about God for the lie of the serpent, and as a result, man worships and serves the creation and *not* the Creator. As Twoists, we believe there is a distinction between the infinitely transcendent and Holy Creator, and the finite, disheveled creation. But the Oneist pagan will have none of it—he won't submit to God and therefore he has to create his own warped version of his existence.

Romans 1 reasons this way: "For this reason,"—because fallen men would rather believe the lie instead of believing the Creator—"God gave them up to degrading passions," or dishonoring lusts, and then Paul explains what those things are.

A couple of quick things.

First, the apostle Paul says three times that God gave them up to something (vv. 24, 26, 28). The wrath given to fallen man is all related to physical things, things related to the body. The body is a forever reminder that while man is on earth, he is not God, and he will die. Of course, one could go the Joseph Stalin route, and reason thusly: "Death solves all problems; no man, no problems."

What Paul insists on is that the wrath of God in the giving over of people to their lusts is itself related to the *material* world. Pagans cannot explain this and as a consequence, they are unable to explain why we should pursue health and holiness in our spiritual and physical lives. Because self-control is forgone, humanists and pagans must treat their bodies with abuse. As a result, they "degrade" their bodies (v. 24). And that's exactly what all forms sexuality (outside the confines of biblical marriage) eventually turn into, especially homosexuality, as explained here, but also every other form of perversion. It becomes a self-inflicted ignominy and degradation. Paul says that bodies are not treated as vessels of holiness, but instead become vessels of lust and impurity. So natural relations are thrown to the side, and unnatural fornication gladly takes its place.

Paul also says that when these things are twisted and bent sideways, which includes all forms of pagan sexuality, they "burn" in their desire toward one another. The word "burn" is *ekkaio*, which comes from two words meaning 'out' and 'burn'. The conclusion is clear: homosexuality, body mutilation through gender bending, pedophilia, bestiality, ecosexuality (when people 'express' themselves in nature), and everything else besides heterosexual one-male/one-female marriage, *results in the burning out of men and women*. It becomes the slow erosion of the image of God, a constant disintegration into darkness and rebellion, and this is exactly the penalty that is due their "error" (v. 27). Since the wages of sin is death, and the sin here is unbridled lust clustering, it follows, then, that the future is nothing but death and darkness for this type of behavior.

What the apostle makes clear here is that unfaithful covenant breakers and blasphemers who wish to jump on the train to *OrgyTown* are given over in reprobation to a depraved mind and as a result, they will do the *insane*. It's a catastrophic *de*volution into failure and impotence.

What is considered shameful and depraved is today paraded in our streets under the guise of 'tolerance' and 'pride'. This reversal of God's law-order is nothing but an attempt of man to follow the logic of his pagan Oneism.

You see, we are living in a time of high-handed rebellion and there's a reason that human sexuality is at the center of it all. Jung said in the 1950's that "We are only at the threshold of a new spiritual epoch." He was absolutely correct. Perhaps he didn't realize the extent of how his ideas would manifest themselves, but the man was a dreamer, no doubt.

The vision of Jung, and especially his foremost disciple, June Singer (who was at his bedside when he died), was all about *the unleashing of the human heart into lust-filled pastures*. The gate was thrown wide open because in Jung's mind, Christianity closes the gate and thus limits the freedom of the individual. Only when that gate is thrust open can one experience the maturity he should experience and explore in his life. "Only when you are free to do as you please can you then be whole," so the thinking went. No doubt the 1960s brought about a spiritual 're-awakening'. Buddhist and Hindu thought flooded the West. The rediscovering of the ancient gods like Osiris and Baal and other fertility cult gods and goddesses led to the inevitable decline in self-government and humility. Instead of mortifying one's flesh, the answer in Jungian terms was to open yourself to it and immerse yourself in it.

Self-fulfillment and self-realization are now done from the *inside*, not the outside, like what we find in a supposedly 'outdated' book like the Bible; and certainly not from the Holy Spirit arresting a man's entire being! Let me explain this as simple as possible: *In Christian theology, sexual restraint out of reverence and love for God and his law-word is a core aspect of the faith.* In Jungian philosophy and psychology, this type of thinking is repressive, unhealthy, and ultimately unhelpful. In order to bring healing to one's soul, and thus illuminate the path of man's humanistic 'sanctification', you simply have to *believe* in fantasy, *pursue* fantasy, and do what Alfred Kinsey said to do: *openly celebrate and market unlimited sexual expression as a basic human right.*

Whether we're talking about temple prostitution in the Greco-Roman world or the urbanites of San Francisco, there is a reason that we always have a connection between a man's religious assumptions and what he does with this body. This is entirely inescapable, and all of it is rooted in man's unwillingness to submit to God.

In his book, *Conversations with God*, Neale Walsch

says that "Hitler went to heaven.... His deeds were mistakes, not crimes. The mistakes did no harm to those whose deaths he caused because they were released from their earthly bondage."

Now, the only way you can rationalize the Holocaust is to adopt pagan thinking. The same is done today with the other sacrament of humanist sexuality: abortion. You hear things like, "Well, these babies would probably grow up poor and unhappy, so it's better this way." This type of thinking is all pagan in origin. The sacraments of fallen man, unbridled sexual expression and abortion, all stem from a refusal to believe the truth about God and adopt the lie: *determining good and evil for one's self* (Gen. 3:5).

In her book, *Androgyny: Toward a New Theory of Sexuality*, published in 1977, June Singer (a disciple of Jung) argues that the future of man must be a sexuality rooted in androgyny (male/female oneness). In order to fully express one's self, and thus bring healing to whatever disorders lie in the sub-consciousness of a person, there cannot be a binary existence; there must be a *Oneist existence*. This conflation is *monism*, which is a core tenant of pagan theology.

In summation: *Jungian psychology opened to door for man to pour out his lusts in any way imaginable.* This most visibly manifests itself in the sacraments of abortion and sodomy. Both things are viewed as a sacred right, a religious ceremony whereby the humanist is able to fulfill his desire to be one with himself and one with the created order.

So, then, what do we do about it? *We preach the law and the gospel.* At every turn, in every opportunity, we must preach. I agree with J. Gresham Machen who said that "the need of the hour is the preaching of the law!"

We must understand that the person who expresses herself in this way is still made in the image God. She is a person God created to reflect him. *She has tried to opt out of that calling by rejecting the law of God, so she must hear the law of God so that she will experience the grace and blessing of shame.* Because the Church has gone the route of antinomianism, the world has followed suit. When Christians forsake the foundation of God's law-word in the Church, why are we surprised to learn that the world wants to forsake it as well?

Therefore, we must be law-saturated, gospel preachers. We must preach God's commandments and statutes, no doubt. But we must also accompany this proclamation with the good news of Christ's death and resurrection and current session as King of kings. We must insist that people forsake their lusts and trade them for the glory of Christ, which is far, far better. We must insist that paganism is destructive and erodes away at image-bearers. We must insist that the only way out of the mess we've created is by repentance and faith—repentance for abandoning God's law, and faith in Christ, whose atonement covers those very lusts.

The humanist gospel in Jungian terms is one of self-realization through fantasy and unbridled ambition. The Christian gospel in biblical terms is one of self-forsaken denial of fantasy and the embracing of the reality of Jesus Christ who is both Lord and Savior. See the difference? For the sake of heaven on earth, *preach*.

FOUR

STATIST EDUCATION: THE DISCIPLESHIP OF FALLEN MAN

The fear of the Lord is the beginning of knowledge;
fools despise wisdom and instruction.

Proverbs 1:7

WHAT SHOULD BE OBVIOUS SO FAR IS THAT there is indeed a great antithesis that spans the course of history, and the two opposing ideas contain radically differing doctrines: *man in rebellion against God vs. man in service of God.* We have, on the one hand, man and his attempts to live life without submitting to Christ, and on the other hand, we have man as a regenerated, recreated being in submission to Christ the King.

This antithesis, this battle against humanism, has been the longest running skirmish in the history of the world. When Satan tempted Adam and Eve with the idea of autonomy—the ability to be a law unto

47

themselves—this historical event was the humanist seed planted in the soil of man's heart. Ever since that moment the antithesis has marched forward in history, the battle between the seed of the woman and the seed of the serpent (Gen 3).

At the core of this struggle is man's belief that divinity lies within himself and divinity in its purest and greatest form finds its *telos*, its end goal, in the state—the ultimate expression of divine man.

In order to address the issue of education, we must start by grasping this great antithesis. Christianity believes in the distinction between the Creator and creation; humanism believes in creation as being divine. As we've discussed already in the previous chapter, this is the Oneism/Twoism view of the world.

Now, because humanism is not ethically neutral, and because it is the religion of fallen, rebellious men, it follows that in order for it to achieve everything it wants to achieve, it has to stay consistent with its presuppositions. As we have seen, the central presupposition within the humanist framework is the idea that divinity is *within* man, most visibly and powerfully expressed in the collective, the ultimate continuity of being, the *state*. But this isn't where it ends. Humanism, which has an eschatology and eye for the future, as well as a doctrinal strategy for achieving that future, will manifest itself in culture through laws and ethics. All worldviews manifest themselves in the world. And it just so happens that humanism does manifest its strategy for the future in a large, expansive way, *the vehicle of statist education.*

Deep within the statist view on education lies the words of Aristotle: the state is "the highest (good) of all, and…embraces all the rest." Don't miss this. Instead of the Church being the *polis*, the true city of God, the state becomes the center of all human life. Because man is seen as divine, the humanist must build some semblance of a foundation, and the foundation that "embraces all the rest" is the state—the unified, collectivist man. Aristotle, in keeping with his presuppositions, famously stated that man is "the best of animals," and is "a political animal." He also said that the citizen "should be moulded to suit the form of government under which he lives." Taking it even further, Aristotle argued the following: "Neither must we suppose that any one of the citizens belongs to himself, for they all belong to the state, and are each of them a part of the state." Statist education has been, and will always be, designed to communicate the following: '*As for me and my house, we will serve the state*'.

As such, we must ask the obvious question: What is the molding process whereby a man can, as a "political animal," be shaped to suit the needs of the collective? Suppose one had a vision for a unified body of divinity on a grand scale, how would you get people trained into that process? Answer: statist education.

Statist education is the discipleship program of fallen men. It is the humanist strategy to achieve the salvation and maturation of man. Education is the anointed messiah; the state is the god she obeys. And what we have here in America right now began with this pagan thinking nearly 200 years ago.

Horace Mann, born on May 4, 1796, is considered to be the chief architect behind the 'common,' or 'public' school system. A Congregationalist minister, Mann labored as a Unitarian under the banner of natural law—that is, the prevailing idea that Nature (not God) gives man certain rights. A leader who considered himself a Christian, Mann was more akin to a religious pluralist. He saw some value in the Bible, but because he started from the wrong premise, he gave himself over to humanism, and thus socialized education.

Mann believed that Nature gives everyone an "absolute right to an education." This entitlement mentality is nothing more than socialism—the belief that the state must give things for free because 'Nature' says so. For Horace Mann, knowledge should not begin with the fear of Lord, but instead knowledge is dispensed through the means of the state. The first chairman of the first State Board of Education in Massachusetts, Mann argued that in order to have a truly free society, the republic needed moral, intelligent people to perpetuate its existence. State-governed education was believed to be the cure-all for society's ills. When people lack education, you get the French Revolution, so Mann argued.

In his own words, Mann said that, "The Common School is the greatest discovery ever made by man." Ironically, for all the hoopla about the common school, Mann could not escape the fact that what he was proposing was an alternative way to be saved—another rival religious training system. Sure, he believed the Bible should be used as a means to promote morality. But he rejected God's law, and thus rejected the notion that one needed to start with the Bible in order to know anything. Education was simply the collectivist means of perpetuating the collectivist vision: a divine state who usurps the God of the Bible. For Horace Mann, natural law took supremacy over biblical law.

In contrast to Mann's doctrines, Calvin's doctrine of total depravity gives men their proper place in the world under God. Mann rejected this notion of depravity because natural law works in conjunction with man; education is thus seen as a means of working alongside man because man's basic nature is one of *innocence*. Total depravity says that a man has sinned against God; Unitarian natural law says that man is broken and simply needs the education of the collective.

Therefore, man is not a sinner, he is basically good—*so they say*. This shift in thinking about education comes to fruition because students are seen as people with "a right to an education" instead of people with a responsibility of obedience before God. It flips the Calvinistic doctrine of man on its head. Man is now free to explore himself in the collective without the repercussions of having to submit to God as an individual as he explores God's world. As Rushdoony pointed out somewhere, public education will always produce statism and anarchy. And anarchy and statism are the *same* thing: both are defections from God and his Holy Law. The difference between anarchy and statism? A politician in a necktie.

Let's examine the key text listed at the start of this chapter. Proverbs 1:7 reads, "The fear of the Lord is the beginning of knowledge; fools despise wisdom and instruction." Along with this text is Proverbs 9:10, which says, "The fear of the Lord is the beginning of wisdom, and the knowledge of the Holy One is insight." And Proverbs 15:33, "The fear of the Lord is instruction in wisdom, and humility goes before honor."

We will add one more verse that is related. Psalm 111:10 says, "The fear of the Lord is the beginning of wisdom; all those who practice it have a good understanding. His praise endures forever."

From Genesis to Revelation, the Bible affirms that

knowledge, wisdom, maturity, and understanding can only come from God. The first and controlling principle of all things is our relationship to God. When the text says that fear is the "beginning," it does not mean that you start here and then leave it behind. No, this controlling principle is a worshipping submission, a holy, reverent fear of the God of the covenant whose name is YHWH. Knowledge, wisdom, and understanding, therefore, in its fullest sense, is a relationship with this covenant God that is entirely dependent and contingent upon him.

When dealing with the issue of education, therefore, particularly the socialistic version of it known as 'public school', we have to start with this presupposition. Since education is the process of bringing someone to knowledge, and since the Bible says it starts with God, it follows then that all attempts at education that do not start with God and a holy fear of him are thus completely and entirely invalid. At best it is an unconscious misunderstanding; at worst they are all rival, subversive claims to divinity and truth.

What Proverbs makes clear in our text, and what the Bible says in places like Deuteronomy 6 and Ephesians 6, is that knowledge, discipline, training, and understanding *begins* with God and is given through the means of God's lawful, covenantal institutions. Education means the impartation of knowledge, and thus, it is an inescapably religious undertaking. There is no neutrality anywhere on this planet, not even in education. The religious presuppositions we bring to the discussion prove where our religious convictions lie. It is either on the side of Christ and his Word, or it is on the side of the humanists and their word. I fear that most Christians today are on the wrong side of the discussion.

Up until the 1830's, American education was Christian. It centered on the institutions of family and Church, and hence it was out of the hands of the state. Due to the influence of Calvinism, the Puritans and Pilgrims built houses and taught their children. *They didn't bring with them a school board, government-controlled standardized testing, and a compulsory, tax-funded budget.* This is because they understood that education was left to the parents and the Church. Training a child started with the fear of the LORD (reading began with knowing the Bible!), and it ended with the same goal. From start to finish, education was the responsibility of the family, and thus the family was free under God to see it through however they wished. In fact, Dr. Joel McDurmon documents in his book *Restoring America* the various ways education was carried out in America before the 1830's: tutors and specialists competing to assist the family.[9] This is what

---

[9] Joel McDurmon, *Restoring America: One County at a Time* (Dallas, GA: Devoted Books, 2019).

free market, non-statist education *should* look like.

But Mann and others like him weren't satisfied. They needed some way to express their collectivist ideology, and the conception of the Common School was the vehicle to do the job.

However, there was one problem: in order to jump on the collectivist train, there had to be a system of paying for it. The connection between socialism and the public-school system lies right here: property tax. Land ownership, which is a biblical concept because God owns the land, not the state, became something the collectivist statists needed to possess and leverage. In the socialist scheme, no one but the state owns land. The 'greater good' takes precedent over individual liberty. Accordingly, in order to pay for the collective schooling system, compulsory taxes were levied against landowners.

You have no doubt heard it said today, 'Taxes are what we pay to live in a free, civilized society'. Or, 'How will we have roads and schools?' You've heard it all; you may have even said such things! This type of thing was also said 200 years ago: 'Don't tell me you care about children when you aren't willing to pay a little tax for the greater good'. This thinking prevailed then, just like it does now.

The problem comes in when we think that public education is an autonomous institution. Education is not a public institution. The public-school system is not an 'it', but a 'they'. There are *people* behind these socialist schemes, and they are people who hate liberty and want more and more funding for their socialist programs. Just ask Bernie Sanders who wants college to be free. How in the world will that get paid? *Taxpayers.* Remember, the government doesn't actually have any money; they have *your* money.

The core problem with the question of education lies in the fact that Christians have given over their responsibilities to the state when the state simply does not have the jurisdiction. This blurring of the lines of jurisdiction is why we are in the mess we're in. The Bible simply does not give the government the permission to educate people. It doesn't. The magistrate is given the sword of justice, and nothing else. And until Christians wake up and read their Bibles, this type of nonsense is going to only get worse. Nothing frustrates me more than the card-carrying NRA member who unwittingly totes his MAGA hat yelling, "Freedom!" all the while insisting on public school education. It's *nonsense* and hypocrisy.

How can Christians possibly believe that teaching knowledge apart from fearing God will produce anything other than death and destruction? How? We are talking about the doctrine of sanctification here, and the collectivist state has one, too.

Sanctification will either be in terms of the Holy Spirit and the outworking of God's law into every area of life, or sanctification will be in the terms of Aristotle: man the political animal is re-made into a servant of the state through the means of statist education. We live in a time when education is heavily financed through legalized theft because it is seen as society's savior and sanctifier, and thus instead of providing social salvation, it has produced social decay. No amount of money will fix this.

How else do you explain the aftermath of a school shooting? When people cry out to their lord and savior to "do something!" What solutions are out there for drugs and guns and such? Education. Education *this*, education *that*. Regulation *this*, regulation *that*. None dare suggest that the Christian faith has solutions, especially solutions to the realm of education.

Make no mistake: Statist education is the discipleship program for humanism, and, on top of this, there are doctrinal concerns for this religious program. What we do not need is prayer back in statist education centers. We do not want prayer in government schools; we want schools to be abolished altogether.

You see, when the state controls something, it creates a *monopoly*. When a monopoly is created, competition is *reduced*. When competition is reduced, *quality goes away*. When quality goes away, you get

America right now.

The entire humanist program is a disaster. *The matter of government school education is easily settled if we can agree that the Bible has something to say about the Lordship of Christ over and in the realm of education.*

And make no mistake, it has a *lot* to say. The truth is, the battle for the future will always be connected to our understanding of the family. Churches will be apathetic and irrelevant as long as the family is entrenched in humanism. Families will be broken up into atomistic pieces so long as education is believed to be neutral. The core of the humanist agenda is this problem of collectivism: a sacrificial offering of liberty and individual freedom for a nebulous, collective 'good'. Our response? By what standard?

Education is a gospel issue. It is a gospel issue because Christ did not die so we could pursue knowledge apart from him and his plan for the world. If the Church will not divorce herself from the collectivist schemes of humanism, the future here in the West will be quite bleak. So, dear parents, teach your children the Lordship of Christ in and through education, and do not be dismayed. It is hard work and there is true sacrifice in doing something contrary to the status quo, but it is the work we are called to do.

FIVE

IMMIGRATION: THE ORGANIZATION OF FALLEN MAN

As for the assembly, there shall be for both you and the resident alien a single statute, a perpetual statute throughout your generations; you and the alien shall be alike before the Lord. You and the alien who resides with you shall have the same law and the same ordinance.

Numbers 15:15-16

GOD HAS A SENSE OF HUMOR. WHEN I LAID out my plan to preach this series, long before it became a book, I did not think that when the moment came to preach this particular message, I would have to do it during a time when the world was watching thousands of Central American immigrants head towards America. In fact, when I first heard about the 'caravan', I chuckled because I knew I was going to be covering the topic. Funny how God works.

Before we dig into the history of immigration here in America and look at what the Bible *actually* says about the issue, I need to make sure we 'clear the air', as it were, with anything a detractor might drum up against me.

It is not an overstatement to declare that the Church at large has refused to teach on the topic. A quick search on Sermon Audio will pull a few messages, but many of the results were radio shows, not sermons. When I typed in 'justification by faith', over a thousand sermons showed up. Clearly the Church is not actually teaching the whole counsel of God like she thinks she is.

Part of the reason for this is because the modern Christian does not believe that political theory is anything to fuss about. Due to the errors of premillennial advocates and the radical two-kingdom troupe, Christians are barred from dealing with these issues because they aren't 'spiritual' topics, and we are supposed to 'just preach the gospel'. This, of course, is a radical Gnosticism that must be rejected because the Bible *does* speak to the whole of life and we must be able to do the hard work of learning and implementing what it teaches.

So, by way of a simple preface: we reject altogether the notion that these topics are 'off limits' because the Christian faith is a *comprehensive* faith—one that touches on every facet of life, especially politics. Besides, immigration has only become a 'political issue' because we have let it become that. The free movement of free individuals is meant to be....*free.* When the state touches it, are we really surprised when it becomes a political issue? This is all because we hate liberty and prefer statism, as we'll see in a bit.

Before we dig into the passage, I want to walk you through a quick history of immigration in the United States so you can see how far we've strayed. All of this information is widely available, and you can find it fairly easy. Keep in mind that the United States Constitution, in Article I, Section 8, Clause #4, says that Congress has the power "To establish a uniform Rule of Naturalization." Don't miss this. *Congress* is granted the power to determine the process of how one becomes a *citizen* of America. This has nothing to do with free individuals visiting, working, or crossing the border into the country. Nor does it give the Executive branch power to do as it pleases.

And now, a brief history.

On March 26, 1790, the *Naturalization Act* was passed. In short, this law limited the naturalization process—the process of citizenship—to free white persons who had good character. In order to know who had good character, they had to live two years in the U.S., and one year in the state of residence, all before applying. This law excluded American Indians, black slaves, and free blacks. (Some states did allow for free blacks to have citizenship). Also contained therein was the citizenship given to children born to U.S. citizens who were abroad at the time of birth.

This act was repealed in 1795, and the one enacted in 1795 was repealed three years later in 1798; and even *that* one only lasted four years before being repealed in 1802. (These repeals were focused on the *timeframe* required before someone could become a citizen; the one in 1798 extended it to 14 years!)

1819 was the first significant federal legislation on immigration. The *Steerage Act* of 1819 established both the reporting of immigration to the U.S., as well as outlined rules for ports and ships and passengers on board.

On July 4, 1864, President Abraham Lincoln signed *An Act to Encourage Immigration*, which was the first act of its kind. This was also Congress' first policy granting them centralized control over immigration. If there was ever a door which awakened the machine of central planning, this was it. The Senate gave the President the power to appoint a Commissioner of Immigration, who was subject to the Department of State. This person could hold office for four years, and the *Act* stated that his salary would be $2,500/year. This was a major step forward in giving the United States government power that the Constitution simply did not give it. (As a side note, the act also gave permission to have in New York City the 'United States Emigrant Office'.)

In 1875 there was direct federal regulation of

immigration which prohibited the entry of prostitutes and convicts. Another major leap forward with regard to the government's control of immigration was the *Chinese Exclusion Act* which was signed into law by President Chester Arthur on May 6, 1882. This prohibited all immigration of Chinese laborers. It was without a doubt a racist attempt at nationalism, which we will touch on later.

In 1891 the Bureau of Immigration was established as the central planning group over the issue. The *Immigration Act* of 1903 soon followed, and it was the next law regulating immigration, this one banning anarchists, people with epilepsy, beggars, and importers of prostitutes.

The *Naturalization Act* of 1906 was passed in Congress and signed into law by Theodore Roosevelt, and it required immigrants to learn the English language in order to become American citizens. It was repealed and replaced in 1940 and modified in 1990.

A few more to consider. In 1917 we had laws and restrictions about people with medical and moral conditions ("illiterates, imbeciles, and alcoholics"), and this also put a head tax of $8 per person on immigrants. The 1920's gave us a quota system whereby it was regulated how many of certain people groups could enter and how many could be in a particular county.

In 1948 we had the first U.S. policy for admitting

people fleeing persecution; it limited 205,000 refugees over two years. It was later increased to 415,000. Two years later, in 1950, Communists were excluded, and subversives were deported. 1952 gave witness to *The Immigration and Nationality Act* which was a sweeping change of statute and brought everything into *one* comprehensive law. It reaffirmed the quota system based on nationality and origin; limited Eastern hemisphere migrants; established a preference for skilled workers and relatives of U.S. citizens; and issued tighter security standards.

The *Immigration and Nationality Act* of 1965, promoted by Ted Kennedy and signed into law by Lyndon Johnson on October 3, abolished the quota system, but still restricted the number of immigrants allowed in the country and thus restricted the naturalization process. Still restricting sexual deviants (like homosexuals), the law opened up the door for more allowance of Asians and Africans.

In the 70's and 80's there was a change in refugee standards, and the next big law arrived in 1986 with the *Immigration Reform and Control Act.* Signed by Ronald Reagan, this law required employers to declare the immigration status of their employees, made it illegal to knowingly hire immigrants, legalized seasonal agriculture workers, and legalized undocumented immigrants who entered the U.S. before January 1,

1982. This amnesty required the immigrant to prove he had knowledge about U.S. history and government; he also had to prove he had the capability to speaking English. (Imagine having to prove your historical knowledge to a government bureaucrat?)

On September 30, 1996, Bill Clinton signed into law the *Illegal Immigration Reform and Immigrant Responsibility Act*. Though dealing in large part with deportation standards, the law also gave authority to the Attorney General to construct barriers along the U.S.-Mexico border.

Since then, we've had several laws regarding amnesty and immigration from certain parts of the world. You may recall, thanks to Republican President George W. Bush, the Homeland Security Act of 2002 which created out of thin air the Department of Homeland Security, who took over control of all immigration enforcement.

There has been various visa reform acts in recent history, and who could forget the *Real ID Act* of 2005 which dealt with identification of individuals. ("Your papers, please.")

Another big one was the *Secure Fence Act* of 2006 signed into law by President Bush. It authorized additional fencing along the Southern border and authorized vehicle barriers, more checkpoints, and lighting to prevent people from, "entering our country illegally."

So that's the history of American law on immigration—in a decently sized nutshell. You should have noticed that over time, central planning took over and the U.S. government was given more and more control. Not only is this entirely unconstitutional, it is completely *immoral*. In fact, many of these laws stem from socialist and racist ideologies. The nationalistic fervor of our country has grown tremendously and judging by the reaction of modern conservatives today (who are simply yesterday's liberals), the vehemence and vitriol over the situation of the caravan is a damning indictment on just how far we have fallen away from biblical law.

And to the Bible we must go.

It goes without saying, since we are Christians after all, that we believe the *entirety* of the Bible. I am going to discuss a lot of different things, mostly from the Old Testament, but that does not mean it is irrelevant or wrong. I also understand that we are not a nation that cares about the covenant of God, and thus we are not a nation that cares about biblical law. But just because we have forsaken Christ the King does not mean that we embrace statist law: *You do not get out of sin by walking away from the solution.* Just because the nation right now rejects biblical law does not mean we abandon it and try and go another direction. So, to the teaching and the testimony we must go.

In Numbers 15:15-16, God laid out some basic concepts regarding biblical law and immigration:

> As for the assembly, there shall be for both you and the resident alien a single statute, a perpetual statute throughout your generations; you and the alien shall be alike before the Lord. You and the alien who resides with you shall have the same law and the same ordinance.

It is assumed that aliens, foreigners, and strangers will be among Israel inside her borders, and they are to be treated a certain way. The way they were to be treated was built on love, and since love is the fulfillment of the law (Romans 13:10), true love is thus a *lawful* love. There was to be one statute—the law of God—for covenant Israel and the alien who sojourns among them. It was to be a "perpetual" statute throughout their generations, and at the end of verse 15, it says, "you and the alien shall be alike before the Lord."

Take extra notice of this up front: there is *one* law for Israel *and* for the alien. According to God's law, God's holy standard, the only way of differentiating between people is the *covenant*, not race, not nationality, not country or flag. There was never a point in time when Israel was defined *exclusively* by bloodline. Because God is the Creator of all people, it follows that all people are accountable to his holy law-word. Which means there is only one legitimate law, and all people are defined in terms of this covenant. The law of God

67

determines who is a covenant member, not race or blood. You could have someone like Ruth the Moabite be a member of the covenant, and have someone like Esau, the son of Isaac, *not* be a member of the covenant (Hebrews 12:16).

Citizenship in Israel was always on a *moral* basis. It was never racial or nationalistic; it was covenantal. Non-biblical law will inevitably place race, ethnicity, and nationality above morality and biblical faith. God's law is ethical; man's law is unethical. The historical motivators that put immigration laws into place was because of socialistic, racist views of man. This collective superiority is the cancer that is destroying the West. And modern conservatives are the ones embracing the nonsense.

All of this stems from two very important points, and these are points that will never be talked about on *Fox News* or *CNN*, and they will be the first two things to go out the window whenever talking to a Republican or a Democrat.

Here's the first one: *The Principle of Ownership.* From cover to maps, the Bible is clear: God is the Creator, and he holds the deed to the earth. The earth is the Lord's, and everything contained therein; and this includes *people*. Leviticus 25:23 reads, "The land shall not be sold in perpetuity, for the land in mine; with me you are but aliens and tenants." Here, God makes it clear that the land belongs to him, and any human who walks on it is a *sojourner*. God owns it, we are called to be covenantal stewards. The land is God's, his covenant people are aliens.

And this is not just about Israel *then*; it's about America *now*. Not only have we forgotten that our ancestors were immigrants, we have forgotten that we are as well. Biblical law should be our controlling principle, not political propaganda. Far too many Christians have attached themselves to the teat of the Republican Party and because of it, they cannot see this issue clearly. They throw this principle of God's ownership out the window and begin to argue in collectivist, socialist terms: 'They are taking our jobs'. Or, 'This is *our* country'. Forget the fact that these are image bearers fleeing from the oppression our nation created; all that matters, then, is '*our* nation'. Ownership thus becomes this illusive, inchoate collective, and instead of biblical law we give ourselves to socialism and racial prejudice.

When we reject this principle of ownership and the priority of God, we create an immigration issue completely out of thin air. Borders in the Bible limit governments, not individuals. Individuals can work, visit, and vacation freely, governments may not. The Bible never gives the civil magistrate the authority to control where and when people go to this place or that.

Their job is to uphold God's law and punish evildoers. Non-criminal individuals are free, under the authority of God's law, to travel and work as they please.

There is also a 'Locked Front Door' fallacy that needs to be addressed because I hear this one a lot. The property that you own (or rent because of compulsory taxation) is yours by God's delegation. It is given to the individual and family. So yes, you can lock your door and shoot anyone who breaks in at night. The land that America occupies is *not* owned by the collective; so no, you may not lock it. Again: who is the owner? This is the question no one wants to talk about. The land is not the front yard of the government! It is *God's* land. And, while we are here, those who own land at the border end up having it confiscated by border agents because there is an urgent 'need' for a wall. (Naboth's vineyard, anyone?)

Ownership is the first principle that is rejected; the second is citizenship, or covenant. We are undoubtedly a nation that had significant Christian influence early on, however, we abandoned that fairly quickly when slave ships were permitted to dock in our ports, and we are now reaping what we have sown. Instead of covenanting with God and abiding by his law, we have developed a nation that rejects God's covenant and has instead embraced nationalism and statism. Remember: *Citizenship in Israel was always on a moral basis. It was never racial or nationalistic; it was covenantal.* Humanist law will inevitably place race, ethnicity, and nationality above morality and biblical faith.

The problem that conservatives refuse to acknowledge, and it makes sense why they refuse, is this issue of citizenship. Citizenship must be covenantal in terms of God, not the state. In ancient Israel, we had a couple of things going on.

First, you had the *sojourner*, who was a naturalized citizen; someone living in the land who was in covenant with God—someone who could partake of the Passover meal. They were circumcised; they adopted the faith of Israel.

Second, you had the *foreigner*, who was someone living in the land who was *not* in covenant with God. They, too, were to abide by God's law and any attempt at subversion would be squashed, because again, there is one law for everyone.

I submit to you that the immigrant issue simply cannot be resolved without understanding covenant.

Though the Constitution gives permission for the government to regulate the process of naturalization, the reality is, it was only a matter of time before this spun out of control. It was only a matter of time before more government regulation came. This is because citizenship is supposed to be covenantal, not nationalistic. The term,

'Illegal immigrant', for example, is a fictional, fiat term derived from unbiblical categories. The only grounds for differentiation between individuals was God and his law; not race, not ethnicity, not nationality, and certainly not man's law. Thus, citizenship is ethical, not national; it was always a matter of obedience to God.

Which is why we need to have an ethical/judicial, that is, covenantal, understanding of immigration. Instead of the talking points of liberals and conservatives, the Church needs to be mature enough to discuss the issues on these terms.

God's law forbade Israel from mistreating the alien/foreigner: (see: Exodus 22:21, 23:9; Lev. 19:33; Deut. 1:16, 10:18, 23:7, 24:14; Mal. 3:5). God's law was intended to protect the alien, but it was also intended to protect the covenant land. Covenant land in Israel could not be alienated because the law of God was and is *fixed*. Covenant curses (Deut. 28:15-68) would confound Israel and the land would vomit them out, just like the Canaanites were vomited out.

Covenant is never solely about ritual and activity; it is also about *location*. God's purpose in man taking dominion over the earth is tied to the actual earth. We think we can divorce ourselves from God in all matters of life; we like to detach God's ownership of the earth and declare ourselves to be the owners. And we are surprised that God is removing the control of the land from his dominion agents? We are surprised that the Church has by and large been lost in the shuffle? Could it be because we have hated our neighbor?

The job of covenant man is to take care of the stranger. Could the problems we face today be because we have forsaken this responsibility? Perhaps it's because we have poorly treated and berated our neighbor instead of befriending and loving her?

The Church's primary combatant right now is not the world, but the Holy Spirit. We have neglected justice and failed to take care of the stranger, and because of it, the Holy Spirit of God has brought sanctions against us using the very law of God we are commanded to obey.

If we are going to disciple nations, you better believe that we are going to have to deal with political theory. If we are going to disciple nations in the manner God says we should, then our political theory ought to be based upon that which God has said in his law-word.

We have to stop making the same mistakes and repeating the same sins that Israel had done. Over and over again, God told Israel to remember that 'such were some of you', and God also told them, 'You are not your own'. This is *covenant*, and this is *ownership*. *Such were some of you*, you were an alien and a stranger at one point. And you are not your own, you were bought by Christ and your job is to serve him, not the state.

Covenant people are people who serve others, not send the national guard to open fire the minute someone crosses the border. Covenant people are people who treat others the way you want to be treated. Pagan slave societies were absolutely brutal; remember Israel in Egypt? There is a reason many left to come to Israel because the law of God in Israel was wisdom in the sight of the nations (Deut. 4).

We are called to welcome the stranger and serve the widow and orphan, not come up with a thousand excuses why we should not. This is the basic ethic of the covenant, and until the Church here in America recovers this ethic, we are going to see ourselves in a lot of trouble—more so than what we already have going on.

The Church has embraced the politics of humanism, without a doubt. Many evangelicals are functional Marxists. Marx was not in favor of open borders and immigration because it never helped his materialistic agenda. When new, entrepreneurial people come into a country, they benefit the economy and create new jobs, thus the central government loses jobs, and control.

The Church has, by and large, been okay with cradle-to-grave security, and the reason conservative Christians want closed borders is because they want more government control. Why? *They don't trust God.* They have been fine with a growing, deficient state, why wouldn't they want to protect that? And for whatever reason conservatives *still* don't understand that in history, it was the socialists and communists who built walls. Remember Berlin?

People say, "You don't believe in the letter of the law, the law of the land?" No. Not when it lacks Holy Spirit infusion. Where the Spirit of the Lord is, there is freedom. Where the Spirit of the Lord is *not* present, there is slavery.

Friends, we have a lot of repenting to do. The gospel of Jesus Christ demands that we love our neighbor and treat the stranger in a manner consistent with how Christ treated us. And if we cannot get this basic requirement of the gospel right, God will visit us with judgment, and you will not be able to say it was unjust.

SIX

WAR: THE AGGRESSION OF FALLEN MAN

When you go out to war against your enemies, and see horses and chariots, an army larger than your own, you shall not be afraid of them; for the Lord your God is with you, who brought you up from the land of Egypt.

Deuteronomy 20:1

IN 1810, FRIEDRICH GENTZ WROTE ABOUT the problem of thinking that the American War for Independence was the fuel for the fire of the French Revolution. Many believed that the two revolutions were the same. Gentz wrote in opposition to this view, citing four main differences.[10]

First, the American Revolution was rooted in a legal tradition with legal principles attached to them; the French Revolution moved on illegal and unprincipled

---

[10] See R.J. Rushdoony, *This Independent Republic: Studies in the Nature and Meaning of American History* (Vallecito: CA, Ross House Books, 1964), pp. 124-125.

77

presuppositions.

Second, the American Revolution was a *defensive* war, a battle fought in order to preserve liberties; the French Revolution was, "from beginning to end, in the highest sense of the word, an offensive revolution."

Third, the American Revolution had an objective which was informed and unwavering—it was *limited* in scope; the French Revolution had no objective, but instead went on because of "arbitrary will, and of boundless anarchy."

Fourth, the American Revolution, because of its limited scope and legal nature, was met with limited resistance; the French Revolution could only "force its way by violence and crimes."

Without a doubt, the American Counter-Revolution, which is what we *should* be calling it (the true revolutionary activity came from the king of England), was utterly and entirely distinct from the French Revolution that happened just a few years later. The French Revolution was built on socialism and the radical ideas of the Enlightenment (thus it was entirely atheist, pagan, and idolatrous thinking that fueled it). The Enlightenment sought to rid God from the equation, and as a result, it elevated man, giving him supremacy over every area of life. This would have massive repercussions for everything from art to political theory, but perhaps the most impact would be in the realm of war.

It is incredibly ironic that the topic of war, like immigration and statist education, is rarely discussed in churches, and the irony being the fact that America has been at war 93% of its entire existence.

Since the birth of our country we have only had 'peace time' for 21 years.[11] Pick any year between this year and 1776 and there's a 91% chance that we've been at war that particular year. According to the *Center*, no U.S. president can truly be considered a peacetime president. We've not gone a single decade without war. The only five-year span we have been without war was from 1935-1940, during the isolationist period of the Great Depression.

From the War for Independence, to constant war with Native Americans, all the way up to wars with Mexico and World War I and World War II, and even to this day with the 'war on terror', our nation is blood-soaked and stained with a history of violence and conflict.

Of course, this is perpetuated because Americans are taxed to their wits end in order to fund the aggressive hunger-lust. According to various websites which are easily found online, in fiscal year 2017, military spending

---

[11] According to the *Center for Research on Globalization*, which you can find online.

was \$598.7 billion. \$178 billion was spent on veterans, and foreign aid came in at \$46.3 billion. This is a total of \$823 billion spent on what is called 'national defense'.

In 2018, all of those numbers increased and the total spent is estimated to be \$894 billion. The budget for 2019 was \$951.5 billion. In 2020 it slated to increase even more. We are literally only two years away from hitting \$1 trillion spent on national 'defense'. All this on a national deficit of \$779 billion this year alone.

Our national debt? According to usdebtclock.org, we're heading toward \$24 trillion.[12] Regarding defense spending, the U.S. accounts for more than one-third of global spending. We spend what the next seven countries in line spend *combined*. We double what the rest of the globe spends *combined*.

More statistics about war come from the June 2014 issue of the *American Journal of Public Health*:

- 90% of all deaths in war are civilians.

- On average, 10 civilians die for every one combatant.

- Also noted was the fact that the U.S. initiated 201 out of the 248 armed conflicts since the end of World War II.

These numbers prove that, without a doubt, *America is a welfare and warfare state.*

So what *does* the Bible teach us about war? Does it

---

[12] Accessed January 3, 2020.

teach us *anything* about war? Let's look at Deut. 20:1–
20, and it's worth quoting at length:

> When you go out to war against your enemies, and see horses
> and chariots, an army larger than your own, you shall not be
> afraid of them; for the Lord your God is with you, who brought
> you up from the land of Egypt. Before you engage in battle, the
> priest shall come forward and speak to the troops, and shall say
> to them: "Hear, O Israel! Today you are drawing near to do
> battle against your enemies. Do not lose heart, or be afraid, or
> panic, or be in dread of them; for it is the Lord your God who
> goes with you, to fight for you against your enemies, to give you
> victory." Then the officials shall address the troops, saying, "Has
> anyone built a new house but not dedicated it? He should go
> back to his house, or he might die in the battle and another
> dedicate it. Has anyone planted a vineyard but not yet enjoyed
> its fruit? He should go back to his house, or he might die in the
> battle and another be first to enjoy its fruit. Has anyone become
> engaged to a woman but not yet married her? He should go back
> to his house, or he might die in the battle and another marry
> her." The officials shall continue to address the troops, saying,
> "Is anyone afraid or disheartened? He should go back to his
> house, or he might cause the heart of his comrades to melt like
> his own." When the officials have finished addressing the troops,
> then the commanders shall take charge of them.
>
> When you draw near to a town to fight against it, offer it
> terms of peace. If it accepts your terms of peace and surrenders
> to you, then all the people in it shall serve you at forced labor. If
> it does not submit to you peacefully, but makes war against you,
> then you shall besiege it; and when the Lord your God gives it
> into your hand, you shall put all its males to the sword. You
> may, however, take as your booty the women, the children,
> livestock, and everything else in the town, all its spoil. You may
> enjoy the spoil of your enemies, which the Lord your God has
> given you. Thus you shall treat all the towns that are very far
> from you, which are not towns of the nations here. But as for

the towns of these peoples that the Lord your God is giving you as an inheritance, you must not let anything that breathes remain alive. You shall annihilate them—the Hittites and the Amorites, the Canaanites and the Perizzites, the Hivites and the Jebusites—just as the Lord your God has commanded, so that they may not teach you to do all the abhorrent things that they do for their gods, and you thus sin against the Lord your God.

If you besiege a town for a long time, making war against it in order to take it, you must not destroy its trees by wielding an ax against them. Although you may take food from them, you must not cut them down. Are trees in the field human beings that they should come under siege from you? You may destroy only the trees that you know do not produce food; you may cut them down for use in building siegeworks against the town that makes war with you, until it falls.

In verses 1-9 we have what we might call, 'Preparation for warfare', and in verses 10-20 we have the 'Rules for warfare'. Regarding the preparation, observe the following: In verse one it is clear that when Israel was confronted with the reality of war, *they needed to trust God above all.* Regardless of the size of the enemy army, they needed to be ruled by a healthy fear of God.

Interestingly, in verse two it is the priest who gathers them together to remind them not to be afraid, but instead trust God above all (v. 3). Why should they trust God in war? Because, as verse four says, the LORD God is the one who goes with them into battle, and it is he who fights.

Deuteronomy speaks about warfare quite a bit:

Chapter 20, 21, 23, 24, and 25 all address the issue. Numbers 1:2-3 tells us that the Israelite army consisted of all males 20 years and older. The older men would be generals and commanders due to the fact that they would have more experience in this type of thing, probably having previously fought in war. We also learn a lot from the books of 1 & 2 Samuel and 1 & 2 Kings.

To quickly summarize some of the principles in preparation for godly warfare:

1. War is done on God's terms per God's orders;

2. The men were to be consecrated and committed to holiness before God;

3. Numbers do not matter; God fights;

4. One of the ways God wins is by confounding his enemies (Joshua 10:10; Judges 4:15);

5. After a war, all of the spoils belong to God because he is the one who wins the battle.

Now, what is easily derived from various portions of Scripture is the fact that this was voluntary conscription. In order to fight a war, it had to be a *defensive* war, and when a defensive war is transacted, courageous men were more apt to want to fight. What man does not want to protect his land, his neighbor, his liberty, and his family from foreign invaders? Because it was done on a voluntary basis—God's law never permits a standing army—this allowed for *conscientious objectors* to decline, and it was also done in such a way as to make sure that both the army was strong, and the family and dominion mandate was still pursued.

In verses 5-7 we see that God's law grants exceptions to voluntary military service. For starters, the man who just built a house and had not yet used it, the man who planted a new vineyard and is ready to reap the benefits for his business, or the man who was just married—they are all to be sent home. Why? *Because the Christian faith is future-oriented.* The task of Godly dominion must go on. Property, family, and business must continue. While some would be eager to fight, they would no doubt have a tendency to be more distracted, and thus they would become a liability for the war. This type of preparation is incredibly important, for it honors the true purpose of life and liberty: the pursuit and priority of the family and the dominion mandate.

The other thing considered in verse eight is the fact that there may be some who are genuinely scared. He may be 'afraid or disheartened'. Not only is he a liability to the objective of the war, he is a liability to his fellow soldiers. Men who are timid and scared are men who will make mistakes in battle.

The last part of preparation is making sure the officers have the commanders put in place so that the organized militia is ready for battle.

A few observations.

We have already seen that the dominion mandate through the vehicle of individuals and the family is of *utmost* priority. We will come back to that principle in a moment. The other thing to consider is that, instead of this being a drafted army under centralized, bureaucratic control, this was a militia: the 'people' coming together to defend themselves, their neighbors, and their homes. *This is not a top-down statist war-machine like what we have in America.* These are men with chests ready to defend themselves, not political pawns meddling in the affairs of other nations.

So that's the *preparation* for warfare. It is a *defensive* fight, and that is the basic rule for what constitutes a just war. The priority is always the carrying out of godly dominion in the land, and this must be protected from external threats. This is not a political ego trip, a 'policemen-of-the-world' type of experiment; it is covenantal conviction.

The next section, verses 10-20, is all about the *rules* while in the war. God's law covers the topic from front to back, start to finish.

In verses 10-15, we see that Israel is in a distant city, outside the land of Israel. They are there because they have been attacked. The first order of business, however, is the offer of terms of peace (v. 10). God's desire is that the kingdom of God be present on earth as it is in heaven, and though war is sometimes a necessary reality, it is not supposed to be a *perpetual* reality. Due to the priority of the dominion covenant being exercised by all men, peace is offered to the enemy instead of imminent defeat.

What happens when the terms of peace are accepted? The nation or people group becomes a subordinate state.

Applied today this would be akin to Kuwait becoming another state in the United States. The reason for this is because nations are not supposed to be the world police. Civil governments are not supposed to meddle in the affairs of other countries. It is immoral for our government to expend lives, money, and property all in the name of the U.S.A. If individuals desire to help, that is another thing—it is not coerced by anyone, it is deeply personal. But bureaucrats in D.C. making decisions about the lives of others is entirely immoral, especially considering the aforementioned statistics.

If, for example, Kuwait, or any other country, desired protective measures from the United States from a perceived enemy, the only way this could be done biblically speaking is for the country to take upon themselves the jurisdictional authority of America. They would have to be grafted in, in order to receive help. Why? Because of this principle found in our text.

Remember: *this is a voluntary conscription.* Men are defending themselves. God has given them the jurisdiction to do so. The outcome of war is not to be nation building and wasted spending, but peace and nation acquisition/discipleship—the expansion of the kingdom of Jesus Christ. Israel was to make all attempts at peace, and part of the peace was taking on Israel's God and law order.

A Christian's theology of war is simple: *peace if possible, dominion covenant at all costs.* If they accept the terms of peace, they become workers, jurisdiction takes over, and they can then be grafted into the political covenant. The conquered city-state becomes a vassal region. But what happens when peace is not accepted? Verse 12 tells us the next step:

> If it does not submit to you peacefully, but makes war against you, then you shall besiege it.

To besiege a place is to cut off its supplies and wait the enemy out. The idea here is the pursuit of forced surrender *without* bloodshed. Again, God's law desires the preservation of life, not the bloodbath that is war.

However, if this does not work and the aggression of the perpetrators begins, an offensive campaign is permitted. Verse 13 says that the men are to perish by the sword (the Hebrew tells us that the 'men' are the *fighting* men, not 3-year-old toddlers), and in verse 14, the women and children and animals are to be "spoil" for Israel. This is payment for the soldiers for their service. Verse 15 is clear: this is to be done for those cities far away.

In verses 16-20, we get a historical glimpse of that which pertained only to Israel in that time, and in that place. There are still general equity principles, however. The armies that dwelt within Israel were to be purged and devoted[13] to God. They were to be destroyed and given the death penalty for their wickedness. Recall that this is in Deuteronomy: Israel had *not yet entered the land*. They were to "utterly destroy" them (v. 17). The reason, of course, is because their iniquity had filled to the brim and God brought judgment to them. The reason God brought judgment was because they did "detestable things" by giving themselves to idolatry. All manner of sexual deviancy was to be purged from the covenant land. The reason, of course, is because Israel may be tempted to do what they do (v. 18), and this would be wicked, a total affront to God.

Some of the other principles we find here are in verses 19-20. When conquering an opponent in a defensive war, fruit trees were not to be cut down. They could use other trees for supplies in order to fight the war, but they were not to destroy the fruit trees. Why? *The dominion covenant matters; the future matters.* The Bible does not permit *total* warfare, the total destruction and annihilation of the land. The productivity of the

---

[13] See Joel McDurmon, *A Consuming Fire: The Holy of Holies in Biblical Law* (Dallas, GA: Devoted Books, 2019).

earth is to be leveraged for the dominion mandate, not for the sad reality of war. At every turn, God's law protects the future and productivity of man, especially in times of war.

You see, war, according to God's law, is meant to be a process of *restoration*. Kind of like how excommunication is intended to be the last straw in getting someone to repent and be restored to fellowship. Since men do not trust Christ who is our only peace, God's law must be wielded in such a way as to promote peace at every turn. Only when the hardness of heart prevents such a thing are men permitted to engage in defensive warfare.

In summation: The Bible says very clearly that we are to have *no standing army*, only voluntary militias; *defensives* wars only, no aggression and meddling; and *peace* as the primary objective. Not world policing and meddling which causes blowback.

The gospel of the kingdom of God with Christ the King at the helm is the deployment of God's law into every area of life. When we consider what it means to disciple nations, we have to keep in mind that no topic is left for the humanists to try and figure out. No area is off limits for the Kingdom, and no area should be ignored. Owing to the fact that Christ died and was raised, we now have, in him, legal representation and responsibility. Sometimes when we talk about these types of things, things like immigration and education, people will not like it; they literally cannot do anything with the meat of the Word. It is like throwing a T-Bone on the lap of a 3-month old. But alas, we press on because the gospel compels us to do so.

Something needs to be said right now, given our context and the things we see happening around us: *The only caravans we need to be worried about right now are the military tanks we line up in other countries around the world.* When fallen men are allowed to express their unbridled aggression and anger, the result is *perpetual* war. America is a welfare and warfare state, and it shows no sign of letting off the gas pedal. We are moving head long into more bloodshed each and every day.

Basic to economic theory is the issue of supply and demand. If you have a standing army, you need a ton of money. In order to justify the spending, you need to create demand. Thus, what do our politicians do in order to create this demand? *Intervene and meddle on a large scale and thus create demand for more military spending.* All in the name of safety and security.

The provisions of safety and security do not come from the state; they come from our covenant Lord who bestows such gifts on covenantally faithful people. There is a reason Jesus said he would never leave us or forsake us. There's a reason the Bible says that God goes before his people to fight for them. *Because safety and security are found in him*—he is our refuge, our rock. That said, fallen man will not be satisfied with this answer. Men resort to violence because the unregenerate heart knows not peace. Apart from Christ, man will always go looking for a fight.

The moment you yank something out of the hands of a free individual and place it in the hands of a collective, that is the moment you have lost. We have handed our individual responsibility to the state in just about every area of life: charity, widows and orphans, education, and especially war. We have stripped our own rights away by allowing politicians and teachers and pastors to let it happen. We have exchanged liberty for protection, all at the cost of more and more money, and more and more bloodshed. We simply cannot tax our way into prosperity, *nor can we drone-bomb our way into freedom.*

So now what? What will God do with a people who have outsourced their individual responsibility? What will God do with a Church that has farmed out their calling? *The outward blessings on our country that we experience right now will turn into a noose around our neck should God choose to ratchet up his sovereign judgment.* To whom much is given, much is required, and when the 'much required' quota is not satisfactory, the judgment comes in to match it. We must do a whole lot of repenting and a whole lot of gospel preaching. And we must trust Jesus and His Word during the process. If the Church is not winning any battles, could it be that God is sanctioning our disobedience? Probably.

SEVEN

DRUG WAR: THE SLAVERY OF FALLEN MAN

You shall not defraud your neighbor; you shall not steal.

Leviticus 19:13a

Neither shall you steal.

Deuteronomy 5:19

IN THIS CHAPTER I WANT TO EXAMINE what has undoubtedly become the single most issue of systemic injustice of our day, and that being the drug war. Now, if I had to guess, I imagine that just about every theonomist has been asked this question in this way… "In a theonomic society, what would ____ look like?" When you have the convictions we have about Scripture, there is a good chance that a family member or friend has come to you and said, "Since you regard God's law as important for a social order, and since you

93

believe it to be thoroughly relevant for providing answers, what does it look like when we think about this or that issue?"

This is a great question to ask. It is a *phenomenal* question to ask. Sadly, it is a question that does not get asked much in evangelicalism today because by and large, we have forsaken God's law, God's standard, and deemed it wholly irrelevant and completely impotent to provide any coherency as it pertains to the issues of today. Many Christians do not first ask the question, "What does God's law say?" because they are trained to search for solutions apart from what God says. Quite literally, the Christian Church here in the West is unable to discern between good and evil because this sort of thing requires that we move on from the milk of the Word and embrace the meat of the Word (Hebrews 5:11-14).

Couple that with an insistence upon the gospel over against the 'oppressive nature of the law', and you get a recipe for disaster. But we reject false dichotomies wholesale and instead find solace in Christ and his law-word. Which means that we *love* the question. We love to answer the question, "In a theonomic society, how should think about *X*? How should we think about education? Politics? Socialism? Drugs?"

That said, we love the question not because we have it all figured out, but because the question itself honors

God. It honors God when we see a problem and appeal to him for the answer. It honors the Spirit's regeneration in our lives when we look for solutions in the very Word he inspired. This means that we value regeneration, and everything flows from it. Ezekiel 36 tells us that God would put his Spirit inside of his people and cause us to walk in his ways. He would take out the heart of stone and replace it with a heart of flesh. He would, quite literally, take the law and *internalize* it—write it on the hearts of his people. We call this being 'born again', and usually this latter part about the law written on the heart is left out of the evangelical equation. To be born again is to love God's law and seek to understand and apply God's law. In Christ, we die to the legal demands of the law—having been crucified with Christ—and also in Christ we receive a new legal status before the law, one which grants us the ability to love it and live within its confines.

Read what David has to say in Psalm 119:97-100:

> Oh, how I love your law! It is my meditation all day long. Your commandment makes me wiser than my enemies, for it is always with me. I have more understanding than all my teachers, for your decrees are my meditation. I understand more than the aged, for I keep your precepts.

This praise comes from the lips of a *regenerated* man.

In other words, since we are gospel people, or more precisely, we are 'gospel of the Kingdom people', we

95

believe it to be important to ensure that we are exercising proper discernment, utilizing the Holy Spirit of God who has taken up residence in us, and doing so by appropriating what God has said in his Word and figuring out how to apply it.

So, what should we think about the drug war? What might God's Word tell us about it? In a theonomic society that is full of regenerated people transformed by the gospel, what might we do about the issue of drugs?

To start, I have to say up front that you are not going to find a Bible verse that says, 'Thou shalt not do drugs'. The modern invention of pharmacological drugs wasn't an issue 2,000 years ago. However, as is routinely the case, understanding what God's law says about *any* issue means that we are going to have to understand abiding principles and a wide range of concepts that span the course of the entire Bible. In short: this is not a matter of looking at one particular verse; instead, it's a matter of putting together some semblance of a systematic so we can properly see the issues at play.

Having said that, let's look at our verses again. Leviticus 19:13a, "You shall not defraud your neighbor; you shall not steal." Deuteronomy 5:19, "Neither shall you steal."

In God's law, there are a lot of ways these two things are stated. There are many verses that declare the objective standard of God's law: We must *not* rob or steal. As discussed in the chapter on socialism, the principle of ownership is embedded within creation. God the Creator owns the world, and everyone in the world—*all* of it belongs to him. He grants a derivative ownership and stewardship to man as man labors in the world within the dominion covenant. Even in his rebellion, God's law still abides and applies. It is still objectively true that an unbeliever ought not to steal from his neighbor. Taking someone's property is *immoral.* Encroaching on someone's person is *immoral.* It is also still objectively true from Scripture that the purpose of the civil magistrate is to enact justice on violations of this sort of thing (Romans 13 gives the magistracy the sword of justice, not welfare or mercy).

Which means, according to biblical law, the only time the state should intervene in the lives of people is when the magistrate is called to hear a case when a victim presses charges and seeks justice for a violation of his life, liberty, and property. The job of the state is to give justice *when a crime has been committed, not create crimes out of thin air.* This has tremendous implications for how we view police, and it also has tremendous implications for how we view the drug war.

I referenced in passing a moment ago Psalm 24:1 which makes clear that all men—pagan or Christian—belong to God: "The earth is the Lord's and all that is in it, the world, and those who live in it." Paul, who no doubt understood this doctrine, declares in 1 Corinthians 6:19-20:

> Or do you not know that your body is a temple of the Holy Spirit within you, which you have from God, and that you are not your own? For you were bought with a price; therefore glorify God in your body.

Speaking of those in Christ, Paul makes it clear that we are not our *own*, we belong to another.

The point I am making is this. When we consider these verses, and the verses about God's prohibition of theft and the oppression of others, then and only then can we can derive a theology of *individual liberty under God*. Individual liberty under God means that a person's life, his actual, physical body, is his property under God. Remember: this is *derivative* ownership. What do we possibly have that we have not received from God? *Not even our bodies*. So, the Bible affirms individual liberty under God, and part of this liberty is, as the Declaration of Independence says, the inalienable right to the pursuit of life, liberty, and happiness (or property, as it was originally coined). Nowhere does God's law permit the state to control men. Since there is one God for the home born and the stranger, only God's law gives the Christian and the unregenerate the ability to coherently understand what it means to be free to pursue life, liberty, and the acquisition of property. The dominion covenant is inescapable! Even the unregenerate made in the image of God pursue these things; they are, however, borrowing (stealing?) from our worldview.

To state it succinctly: *God's law grants us derived ownership over our life, over our liberty, and over our property, and this is true for all image bearers of God.* When we have this biblical presupposition from God's law in place, we can now deal with the question of the drug war. It is my contention, and I believe it is the Bible's contention as well, that based on the principle we just stated, *the state has no business controlling what we put into our bodies, and thus has no business waging this war.* The statist backed war on drugs has done nothing but destroy freedom in this country.

The drug war, which began in 1971 when Richard Nixon signed into law the Controlled Substances Act, was actually a war on freedom and a war on minorities. Since 1971, we have spent over $1 trillion to fight the drug war, to create out of thin air a new category of non-violent crime. At the center of the act was the power given to the Food and Drug Administration (FDA) and the Drug Enforcement Administration (DEA) to determine which drugs would receive which scheduling. The government had long ago determined to control the *food* industry, now they wanted the *drug* industry. In 1906, the Food and Drugs Act was signed by Theodore Roosevelt and was the first in a series of what we call 'consumer protection laws'. (See? You're the consumer and you need to be protected by government agents.

You're welcome.)

At any rate, the United States government has had an interest in food and drug for a long time and this continues to be the case. Listed on the Schedule I DEA drug prohibition catalog is marijuana. Also listed is heroin, LSD, and ecstasy. On one level, it is entirely laughable that marijuana is on the list with these drugs. It is a plant, and, contrary to government reporting, it does not impair you like alcohol. The fact that it is on this list with heroin and LSD is indicative of the government's collective ineptitude and idiocy.

On another level, the fact that we have a list like this is yet again proof that our government overlords are doing this for more than the stated reasons. This is *not* done to 'protect people from hurting themselves', this is done in order to pay the bills of the corrupt criminal justice system. But I'm getting ahead of myself.

A couple things for your consideration:

- 81% of all drug arrests are simply for *possession*. You can be handcuffed, your car can be impounded (civil asset forfeiture is a lucrative business, by the way), and you will go bankrupt, all for the fact that you had a bag of plant in your pocket.

- In 1980, 580,900 people were arrested on drug-related charges. By 2014, it increased to 1,561,231. More than 700,000 in 2014 were related to marijuana. With regard to federal prisons, just about half are incarcerated for drug-related charges.

- One estimate said that, by ending the war on drugs, we could save $41.3 billion dollars a year—maybe even closer to $50 billion.[14]

We would take away tens of millions of man-hours spent in courtrooms, office buildings, police departments, and paper trails accumulated by all of them. Yet, there is another aspect to this.

The war on drugs is without a doubt a systemic injustice as it pertains to minorities, especially blacks and Hispanics.

Look at these statistics:

- In 2010, we had 1.6 million people in state and federal prisons; that's less than 1% of the population. [What if we separate this out by race?] Whites make up 64% of the total population, 31% of the total incarcerated. Blacks make up 14% of the total population, 36% of the prison population. Hispanics are 16% of the total population, but 24% of the prison population. [This is absolutely astounding.]

- Out of young, black males, 1 in 4 go to jail. [Quite literally, as one study put it, if you're a young, black male, you're more likely to go to jail than get married or go to college.] 1 out of every 11 blacks are in prison.

This is *systemic* injustice, *racial* injustice, and it is a problem that we the Church are called to address.

Even so, do we see the problem? Might we agree with someone like Louis Farrakhan? Regardless of what you might think of him, he articulated the systemic

---

[14] You can easily find these statistics online.

racism involved in the drug war when he said in 1990, "There is a war being planned against black youth by the government of the United States under the guise of a war against drugs." He is absolutely right. So, now what?

The reality is, the drug war is modern-day slavery; it is kidnapping in every sense of the word. Slavery has moved from the plantation to the prison system, and the drug war has been the vehicle to do it. In light of this truth, we are Christians, and we confess that the state is a *terrible* savior. "Why doesn't the government do something about XYZ?" is a terrible way to start finding solutions.

You see, the humanist state has to create some sort of sanctification. They have a view of man, and their view is that man includes being managed by *other* men. This usually involves arbitrary rules and bearing false witness; creating laws in order to generate funds to oppress minorities. It involves corruption in the police force and corruption in the courts. Man must be locked in a cage for possessing a drug, and *then* can he be sanctified.

However, law enforcement does nothing to provide man with moral character and self-control. *This is salvation by law.* The systemic injustice we see in our culture is a result of men doing the humanist thing instead of the biblical thing. Salvation by law does not work, nor can it ever work. Nevertheless, this is the only thing humanists know. What the humanist calls mass incarceration, we call kidnapping and abduction. Concepts matter, and the ability to discern between good and evil matters. And the only way we're going to accomplish *that* is by calling the thing what it is: modern slavery. Salvation by law. Kidnapping. Injustice. And so on.

Conservatives today will decry the welfare state on immigration, but they will ignore the drug war. Why? *Because it doesn't bother them.* It doesn't actually mess with them. That is a 'black community problem', they say. Listen: You cannot complain that the black community is fatherless, all the while cheering on your local police department as they create crime out of thin air. You cannot criticize the fatherlessness when you are cheering on the system that puts fathers in prison unjustly.

A government agency controlling something over *there* will quickly become another government agency controlling something over *here*. This is because we are not looking to Christ for sanctification. The age-old dialectic is this: how do we maintain liberty without liberty getting out of hand and causing problems with everyone? The only answer is individual liberty *under God.*

Government controls on things like drugs and soda pop should not be seen as necessary measures to ensure that we, the patients, are being taken care of by our doctor-nanny, the state. No, we should see this as the state being criminals and *we are the victims*. If addictions and crimes are reduced all the way down to mere medical problems, then we have a complete revolution in our understanding of man and sin.

If we are going to worry, we should probably be worried about the state government running everything, not drugs. *Criminal law is supposed to protect us from others, not ourselves.* What a man puts in his body is *his prerogative only*, not the prerogative of the state who tries to be omniscient.

Back to the question about God's law and what it would say about the drug war. *In a truly free society, a truly theonomic society, what a man ingests and grows becomes a concern for the civil magistracy when a crime is reported, and real victims, corroborated by two or three witnesses, are produced.*

When someone is deprived of life, liberty, and property, the *aggressor* is the criminal, the deprived one the victim. When a government agent deprives someone of life, liberty, and property, we say, 'They are just doing their job and enforcing the law'. This is wicked, and this is rebellion. A culture that revolts and rebels against God and his law-standard is a culture that is bent on suicide. *That* is why this injustice has created such problems in our society.

If a man does not have liberty, he does not have purpose, and thus he has no reason to live. But man does have a purpose in Christ, underneath the dominion covenant, and it is our job to see to it that not only are we in obedience to it, but that our neighbor is as well. The drug war is a gospel issue because the drug war is injustice made manifest. There is *idolatry* attached to the injustice, and if we're going to preach the gospel, we must *speak*.

EIGHT

GUN CONTROL: THE STATIST PROTECTIONS OF FALLEN MAN

You shall not murder.

Exodus 20:13

If a thief is found breaking in, and is beaten to death, no bloodguilt is incurred; but if it happens after sunrise, bloodguilt is incurred.

Exodus 22:2-3

I IMAGINE THAT AT THIS POINT YOU have probably caught on to something important as it pertains to our battle against humanism, and that is the fact that the greatest expression of humanism can be found in the collective, statist regime. Echoing the Tower of Babel, when men try to make a name for themselves, the path they will inevitably choose each and every time in order to accomplish this lust is the Power State. In lieu of the fact that fallen men desire the path

107

of the Enlightenment—the complete rejection of God—we should note that they will always prefer the power religion. The power religion goes with the power state, and together they believe that might makes right; that those at the top are in positions of authority because they are stronger. Those at the bottom are to simply submit to them because the all-knowing, all-seeing state is their lord protector. Some call this survival of the fittest, the Bible calls this idolatry.

In each chapter we have considered the various doctrines of humanism, what we call the *politics* of humanism, and each chapter we have to one degree or another talked about the role of the civil magistrate. Whether it's sexuality, education, war, or immigration, this is important to know because the civil magistrate *does* play a major role in a society. I am not arguing for the complete eradication of civil rulers—an anarchist dream. The covenantal jurisdiction of the magistrate is laid out by God in various places of Scripture, most notably being Romans 13. So, I very much appreciate and respect the role of the magistracy. I believe that having a sound, ethical justice system in place is incredibly important. I believe the Bible teaches us a lot about due process, the role of the jury, and the role of witnesses. However, I do not believe the state can and should be given unending power, nor do I see the state as being a suitable replacement for God. Consequently, the state must be prophetically rebuked and brought back inside its proper jurisdiction—and Scripture demands such a view.

We do what we do because we believe this to be a *gospel* issue. The way the magistracy is carried out must be consistent with Christ our King. Kings and rulers of the earth are commanded to pay tribute to Christ in their rule (Psalm 2), and since they have been given the sword of justice, this rule must be done in accordance to what God says. To say that this has nothing to do with the gospel of the Kingdom is to truncate the gospel and hand the house keys over to the humanist. And this we must *not* do.

In this chapter I'm covering the issue of gun control, which is undoubtedly the statist protections of fallen man. Owing to the fact that humanism relies on man to be the determiner of good and evil (rather than trusting Christ), the fallen man must figure out a way to make sure his constituency 'falls in line'. *In order for the collective to succeed, the individual must be eradicated.* There is no room for man to have liberty, and there is no room for man to determine righteousness based on God's law. This means that men are stripped of their individual right and duty to defend life, liberty, and property. These biblical principles are yanked out of the free man's hands and put instead in the hands of bureaucrats and police. As Christians who worship the Lord Jesus Christ, this will not suffice.

Whenever we have a school or church shooting, many of those affected by this terrible tragedy cry out to the savior-state, saying things like, "Why won't the President do something!?" Or, "Congress must act *now*." The highest appeal they can come up with is the all-knowing, all-seeing state. From the state, it is perceived, comes salvation and restoration—a humanist worldview.

Speaking after the Orlando nightclub shooting a few years ago, President Barrack Obama offered his condolences to the victims and ended his speech by saying:

> This massacre is therefore a further reminder of how easy it is for someone to get their hands on a weapon that lets them shoot people in a school, or in a house of worship, or a movie theater, or in a nightclub. And we have to decide if that's the kind of country we want to be. And to actively do nothing is a decision as well.

A year later, in June of 2015, President Obama responded to the shooting at a church in Charleston, South Carolina by ending his speech saying, "We don't have all the facts, but we do know that, once again, innocent people were killed in part because someone who wanted to inflict harm had no trouble getting their hands on a gun."

Now, liberals will shout at conservatives and say, "Guns must be banned! We're tired of the shootings!" Conservatives will say, "Come and take them! Guns don't kill people, people kill people." The political rhetoric is oftentimes completely insufferable, and as Christians who follow the Lord Jesus Christ, Christians who are commanded to teach the nations how to obey Christ, we must offer something better than this. To the teaching and the testimony, we must go. What are we to think of guns? More precisely, what are we to think of self-defense?

The sixth commandment says, "You shall not murder." The King James Version says, "Thou shalt not kill." The word for murder, or kill, is *ratsach*, and it carries the idea of *premeditated* killing. It is unjustifiable murder, the unlawful taking of innocent life. This is *unjust* violence towards someone. Things like capital punishment, self-defense (as we'll see), and even just war are *not* included in this commandment because God's law draws distinctions between these things. We need to understand that this is the *negativism* of the law—you shall *not*. The positivism of the law is the reverse: you *shall* protect/defend life. God's prescription for what it means to be Kingdom people is for us to defend the lives our neighbors and families. We are to live peaceable lives (peace is a fruit of the Spirit), and we do this not only by refusing to be oppressors, but also standing up for the oppressed.

We each have a responsibility as individually free men and women to seek to prevent the injury and assault of others. When we refuse to protect the defenseless, *we are refusing to obey God.* This means that each of us are called to be a police force. We are not to farm out our obedience to the sixth commandment (or any other commandment for that matter) to bureaucrats with uniforms and guns. As Rushdoony pointed out:

> The law asks two things of every man, obedience and enforcement. To obey a law means in effect to enforce it in one's own life and in one's community. God's law is not a private matter; it is not for us to obey personally simply because we like it, meanwhile leaving other men to follow whatever law they choose. The law is valid for all; to obey it means to accept a universal order as binding on us and upon all men. Obedience therefore requires that we seek a total enforcement of the law.[15]

What Rushdoony is arguing, and what we must insist upon, is a decentralized, individualized responsibility for justice, not a collective one which strips man of his individual responsibility. Each person has a police power, and in order to have a godly social order, we must each take responsibility in defending each other. This is simply what it means to love your neighbor as yourself. To love your neighbor isn't to just *not* murder him; it's also the seeking out and arresting of the murderous assailant, ensuring that he is put on trial and condemned to death for his crime against his victim and against God. Loving God and loving neighbor

---

[15] R.J. Rushdoony, *The Institutes of Biblical Law, Volume 1* (Philipsburg, NJ: P&R Publishing Company, 1973), 220.

requires this of us. The gospel absolutely compels us to seek justice for our neighbor. That is *love*.

In Exodus 22:2-3, we have laws of restitution and there are two examples given of what true self-defense looks like:

> If a thief is found breaking in, and is beaten to death, no bloodguilt is incurred; but if it happens after sunrise, bloodguilt is incurred.

There are two scenarios, both dealing with a thief looking to steal, but there are two differing situations. In verse two we have a thief caught breaking into a home. The Hebrew is literally "digging in," as in, digging through the mud walls of an ancient home.

The context here is pretty straightforward: He's in the process of entering a home that does not belong to him, and he's digging in somewhere around the house. The homeowner is alerted to the threat and responds with lethal force. The Bible here teaches the principle of self-defense: *the right and responsibility to protect one's self and his family from imminent harm and danger.*

Nowhere in this verse does it say that it is *dark*. We know from Job 24:13-17 that evil is more comfortable doing its bidding at nighttime. That's pretty clear. But note that our text here does not tell us that it is dark. Many commentators simply assume that the difference here is nighttime or daytime. I don't think that's the main point here.

Now, while we are here, I should say that it's not *terribly unreasonable* to assume that in verse two, we're talking about a nighttime break-in. However, I don't think this is painting the whole picture. In verse three it says, "But if it happens after sunrise," which literally means, "The sun shone on him," there "will be blood guiltiness" on his account.

As I was studying this, I noticed that pretty much all of the commentators I looked at believe these two verses to be *parenthetical*. Calvin himself thought it was just a side note in an otherwise string of comments. It's as though Moses wrote verse one, snuck in a quick footnote here in verse two and the beginning of verse three, and then went back on his happy way at the end of verse three. I don't think Calvin is correct in saying this is parenthetical. I think it *does* tie into verse one and the rest of three and the next few verses.

Gary North doesn't really say anything about these verses in his *Tools of Dominion*, and Rushdoony said very little in his commentary. I guess I'll offer up my thoughts!

The normal interpretation is this: when it's dark, and a thief breaks in, you can defend yourself and if the perp dies, you are not to be charged with murder. You were simply defending your 'castle'. (Castle doctrine is rooted in this verse). This is true, and good, and right. It is very much consistent with Scripture. Then, it is normally taught, if it is daytime, and a thief is breaking in, you have to make sure you are not shooting your cousin Vinny who was just trying to make a sandwich. Poor Vinny if it's nighttime! This is the normal interpretation. When it's dark and a thief is breaking in, he's assuming that someone is home, and is therefore more liable to injury. When it's daylight and a thief is breaking in, he's assuming that probably no one is home and therefore isn't as liable to injury. In daylight, you have a more reasonable chance to confirm the threat to your life, so it's believed.

But I'm not happy with this normal interpretation. I think it's correct, and I think there is good sense in thinking this, but it just doesn't connect to the context really well. Here's what I mean.

The context is established in verse one: we're talking about theft.

> When someone steals an ox or a sheep, and slaughters it or sells it, the thief shall pay five oxen for an ox, and four sheep for a sheep. The thief shall make restitution, but if unable to do so, shall be sold for the theft.

The first verse describes what happens when a thief steals something and then sells it: he's to pay it back five-fold or four-fold, depending on the animal. *But the context doesn't change; we're still talking about the thief.* Remember: (not to insult your intelligence dear reader), *thieves steal property.* Don't miss the context.

115

If he breaks into a house, he has crossed the threshold—he was not invited, and, interestingly enough, the crime of theft had *not yet been committed*. The man was *attempting* theft: he's found digging into the walls, and thereby positions himself in harm's way. He was on his way to commit a crime and since people don't normally just start digging an entrance in the side of the house at 2am, the reality is, the man's intentions aren't entirely clear. If we say it's dark, and again that's probably the case, we don't know what kind of harm he's seeking to inflict. Is he there to take some money? Is he there to steal a sandwich? Is he there to destroy the family? Perhaps he wants to add an addition to the house at no charge? *Discerning his intention is nearly impossible;* you cannot do so when the threat is immediate and in the middle of the night. We do not know and therefore do not have the time or context to wait and see. He is bent on committing a crime and potentially hurting the man or his family and is thereby liable to destruction. There is no 'blood guilt incurred'.

But this is where it gets interesting. In verse three, we have a different situation. Again, we don't know if it was dark in verse two. Even if it *isn't dark*, and someone is breaking in, a man has a right to defend himself and his neighbor—the protection of life in the sixth commandment backs him. However, in verse three it says, "But if it happens after sunrise."

116

I think we're dealing with a thief who has *already committed the crime*. Going with the presupposition that it *was* dark in verse two, which is good and fine and most likely the case, verse three explains what happens when the sun has shone on the criminal, meaning that we can assume he stole something at night, but the morning has come and the crime has been committed. I think what we're looking at here is a situation *after* we know a crime has been committed. The thief is made in the image of God and is therefore *not* to be killed—for this is not the proper measure for the law. Instead, the rest of verse three—which defends my thesis—says that he's supposed to make *restitution*.

This isn't simply a story about a thief breaking in at night over against a thief breaking in during the day; this is about a thief who is attempting to commit a crime over against a thief who has *already* committed the crime. Self-defense applies in the daytime or nighttime. And yes, in the day we can literally see things better than at night, especially in mud homes without electricity! The point God's law makes is that regarding the crime of theft, the thief does not receive the death penalty. You can't just kill a thief; this is not the position of biblical law. You can and should and are commanded to *defend yourself and your family from the intentions of a criminal*, which are oftentimes unknown. But you can't just kill a thief because he stole something—he must make restitution.

Now, why bring all of this up. As I said before, the Bible says we're to love God and our neighbor. We are supposed to value God above all, and in light of *that* we are supposed to value our neighbor's life. This is the summation of the law of God, and this is what gospel people do. When we're transformed by the Spirit and the gospel message has taken us captive, we live a certain way. We live inside a social order a certain way. And the way we live is informed by God's law. The issue of gun control falls right into this paradigm.

Stated as plainly as I know how, *gun control removes the right and duty of citizens to protect themselves not just from murderers and those seeking to do harm, but government officials who desire a statist hell.* Now, I'm not going to get into the whole automatic weapon ban and whatnot (still a violation of the second amendment, and we should have them because the state shouldn't have more firepower than us). However, I'm very much in favor of a society saturated by the gospel to such a degree that men beat their swords (guns) into plowshares. That's because I'm a postmillennialist. *But I also know that there are people who legitimately want to do harm.* Even still, you don't solve the problem of people wanting to do harm by removing the one thing the man has: *self-defense.* Disarming a populace, or, in our case, restricting the populace from having military grade weapons, and thus giving police those weapons, isn't going to solve the issue. When the government says you can't have a gun, you don't just need a gun, you need a loaded one.

The gospel is supposed to change people, and it is the gospel that gives a man self-control. That's the *only* way the problem is solved. In the meantime, the Bible gives us a right to defend life, liberty, and property; to defend our own person, our family, and our pursuit of the dominion mandate.

Which means that it is imperative that we plan for the future and have a plan to protect that plan for the future. We are not arguing over the second amendment, though we do believe in it and ought to defend it. We're Christians, *first*, which means that we want to defend the lives of our neighbors.

Practically speaking, if you don't own a firearm, you should plan to get one. If you don't know how to use one, learn. If you don't have a plan to protect yourself or your family, get one—fast. Get trained on situational awareness so you know what's happening around you at all times. Go to the gun range. Learn about how to prepare for sudden emergency situations. Study on how to use a gun in a way that obeys the Bible. Learn how to switch out a magazine quickly. We cannot think that we are obeying the sixth commandment simply by refraining from killing someone; no, obeying the sixth commandment means you better know how to protect the life of your neighbor when she's threatened…so get a gun and know how to use it.

And parents, when thinking about the future, *we need to be teaching our children the biblical obligation to resist unrighteousness and rebel against tyranny.* God forbid we Christians find ourselves in a defensive war against our own nation, but it wouldn't be the first time. Therefore, we plan and prepare, and in the meantime, we must be zealous about the preaching of the gospel of the kingdom of God and the self-control and defensive posture that comes with it. Christians are actually the ones here to serve and protect.

NINE

RACISM: THE PREJUDICE OF FALLEN MAN

So God created humankind in his image, in the image of God he created them; male and female he created them.

Genesis 1:27

After this I looked, and there was a great multitude that no one could count, from every nation, from all tribes and peoples and languages, standing before the throne and before the Lamb, robed in white, with palm branches in their hands. They cried out in a loud voice, saying, "Salvation belongs to our God who is seated on the throne, and to the Lamb!"

Revelation 7:9-10

THE TASK BEFORE ME IS RATHER daunting. Sure, there's a lot that *could* be said about racism, and no doubt when I'm done, I will probably regret that I didn't say more about this or that. That's just the nature of preaching and writing anyway.

121

However, that's not the 'daunting' I'm talking about. The reason something like this is daunting is because when we pause and consider American history, *I don't think that most white people realize the depths of damage that has been done to black image bearers.* I, for one, will be first in line to admit that up until a few years ago, I had no real idea the depths of racism in our country. I was taught in public school that Lincoln freed the slaves, the south was full of racists, and that we should thank God the North came to save the day.

I was also taught that slavery wasn't *that* big of deal, *really*. Sure, in hindsight we probably shouldn't have done that, but it wasn't as awful as people make it sound. Dismissive beliefs like these are the types of things I learned, and I'm pretty sure that I'm not the only one who was taught to think like this!

Growing up in Southern Michigan, which was predominantly white, I had no real hatred towards those who looked different than me. I never really spent time dwelling on this fact. It wasn't that I perpetuated the 'color blind' theory, either; I guess the Lord just kept me from that sort of racial prejudice.

In 2004, I moved to inner-city Philadelphia to complete my bachelor's degree. I had a job in North Philly working at a window manufacturing company whose employee roster included lots of different people: some African Americans, many Puerto Ricans, a few whites. In fact, the eclectic company had an owner who was Korean. It was in this environment that I learned more about *culture*—something way different than my experience in rural Michigan. Perhaps the highlight of my experience in Philadelphia was a friendship that was kindled while in seminary with a black pastor from New Jersey, with whom I still keep in touch today. One time, for an assignment, I had to attend a black church in South Philly and on that particular Sunday, I was the only white guy. *I loved it.* The class was about immersing ourselves in a different culture, to truly 'reach out a hand' towards our brothers and sisters of a different ethnic background. It was a tremendous joy doing this, and something I'll *never* forget.

By God's grace I learned a lot in my experience, and I share this because 1) I know that my story is unique, and only I can tell it; 2) Not everyone has this sort of experience; and 3) To give testimony to how we might fight against the sin of racism in our day.

Racism is the prejudice of fallen man. It is the hatred and poor treatment of those different than you. It isn't just personal, it is systemic. In our context, it isn't simply a disdain for someone of a different ethnic background, it's done by those in the *majority* towards those in the *minority. Racism inherently believes in ethnic superiority.* By its very definition, the racist believes himself to be genetically superior to those in the minority. This type of thinking is pagan in origin, is rooted in materialistic determinism, and goes against the Bible as we'll see.

In our culture today, particularly here in America, we have varying degrees of understanding as it pertains to racism. We have whites who acknowledge that racism is a real thing, have repented of their racist views of other minorities, and are genuinely trying to move forward. We also have whites who refuse to acknowledge that racism is a thing, refuse to see why we should 'cater to minorities', refuse to acknowledge that white privilege is a thing, and want nothing to do with reconciliation. Conveniently, they reject the idea that systemic racism and injustice exists. After all, the past is the past, right? Slavery was abolished 150 years ago, right? Jim Crow is gone, right?

In large part, many that I know are in the first camp. I don't believe I know anyone in the latter category, at least not personally. But there is also another category to consider: *whites who just don't know.* They aren't hostile, they are stuck. They know there are problems, but they aren't quite sure what to do about them. They are open to learning, eager to try to understand, but aren't sure where to go from here. I'm going to do my best to address all three with the hope of ensuring that we are true to our calling to be *ministers of reconciliation.*

When prepping to preach this sermon two years ago, I read two important books that were recommended to me. The first was *Woke Church* by Eric Mason. The other was *Dream With Me* by John Perkins. I also recommend that you read *Slavery in Christian America* by Joel McDurmon. This is another great book which gives the true story of the American chattel slavery system.[16]

As a Christian, and especially as a Christian Reconstructionist, I am convinced without a doubt that systemic racism not only exists, but it is *devastating* our nation. We have systems in place right now in America that oppress minorities and these socialist systems do *nothing* but perpetuate injustice. So, it *does* exist. In fact, not only *does* it exist, I am convinced that the Bible—through the means of God's law—can *actually address the problem.*

As redeemed Christians who take the Lordship of Christ seriously, and take God's law seriously, we very much ought to believe in the pursuit of justice as being integral to what it means to be a Christian. God's law at every turn demands justice for the weak, the oppressed, and the downtrodden. But justice cannot be done purely

---

[16] Eric Mason, *Woke Church: An Urgent Call for Christians in America to Confront Racism and Injustice* (Chicago, IL: Moody Publishers, 2018). John M. Perkins, *Dream with Me: Race, Love, and the Struggle We Must Win* (Grand Rapids, MI: Baker Books, 2017). Joel McDurmon, *Slavery in Christian America* (Dallas, GA: Devoted Books, 2019).

on socio-economic considerations. This is why social justice—a term that belongs to Christians, and we shouldn't be afraid of using it—is seen as being a form of socialism. Justice must always be in terms of God's law, for that is the only true and abiding standard. For example, asking the government to pay more money in welfare isn't justice. People *think* it's justice because, after all, this would help people, right? *Wrong.* Welfare belongs to the individual, the family, and the Church—*not* the state.

The Bible address racism in several places, but I chose two sections of Scripture to shape this chapter. The first is found in Genesis 1:26-28:

> Then God said, "Let us make humankind in our image, according to our likeness; and let them have dominion over the fish of the sea, and over the birds of the air, and over the cattle, and over all the wild animals of the earth, and over every creeping thing that creeps upon the earth." So God created humankind in his image, in the image of God he created them; male and female he created them. God blessed them, and God said to them, "Be fruitful and multiply, and fill the earth and subdue it; and have dominion over the fish of the sea and over the birds of the air and over every living thing that moves upon the earth."

The second text is found in Revelation 7:9-10:

> After this I looked, and there was a great multitude that no one could count, from every nation, from all tribes and peoples and languages, standing before the throne and before the Lamb, robed in white, with palm branches in

their hands. They cried out in a loud voice, saying, "Salvation belongs to our God who is seated on the throne, and to the Lamb!"

From start to finish, the Bible has a vision for humanity—a plan for history and man inside of history, and it starts with this principle: *all of mankind is made in the image of God*. This is basic Christianity. Men and women of all tribes, tongues, and nations are equally created in the image of God, which means that both are glory-bearers and glory-reflectors. Man is meant to reflect the nature and character God—though limited in many ways—and in so doing, bring the world into subjection to Christ. When God created Adam and Eve, and thus the nations, the calling of the dominion covenant was given. Black, white, Hispanic, or Asian, the calling is clear. Dignity, value, and purpose are imprinted on *all* men and women, because *all* bear the image of God.

Now, we know that after the fall this image became tainted and fractured. The image was broken, we became legally and ethically disenfranchised from the covenant Lord. We became dead in our sins and rebellion, for we had transgressed the law of God, and because of it, we were cursed.

However, what needs to be said here is that this was an ethical/judicial curse. The curse wasn't that some of us had to be Caucasian, some had to be black, and others had to be Latinos. That's *not* the curse. The curse is the fact that we broke the law of God, are now guilty of violating the covenant, and all tribes and tongues are now in need of repentance and faith in Christ. The so-called 'curse of Ham' is just as erroneous as the Black Hebrew Israelite nonsense. Both are trying to solve a problem with the wrong presupposition.

For the Christian who understands his Bible, the problem is sin, and the solution is the cross of Christ. This is why we reject materialistic determinism: the thinking that genetics is the underlying issue. The problem isn't skin color or ethnicity, the problem is sin; and the solution is the gospel. Which means that in Christ, *these things are resolved.* In Christ, the man who used to hate blacks can now be forgiven. In Christ, the black man whose oppression led him to develop erroneous views of his oppressors can now be forgiven. In Christ we are equally and ultimately *many* and *one*— there is no Jew or Greek, all are unified in Christ.

This is where Revelation 7 comes in. The great goal of history is the unity of man in Christ before the Throne of God. There is no black/white separation like what happened during the Jim Crow era. It's not as though we have one section of this great new city in the new heavens and new earth over there, and all the Chinese Christians will be there, while over yonder is the black church, and over here is the white church. No, *all will be in unity together before the Lamb of God.*

Which means—please hear me—that we must work *backwards* from this end goal. And how do we work backwards from this grand vision of unity between all peoples? This is where I want to spend the rest of our time.

In his book *Woke Church*, Dr. Mason spends a whole chapter discussing the biblical concept of lamentation. Lamenting ought to be practiced by Christians, but this doesn't mean we just vent and complain. *Lamenting is the heartfelt process of going before God being emotionally undone.* This is us agreeing with God in mind, heart, and soul about the circumstances in question.

Mason lists[17] the things that should be lamented, and I agree with them:

1. ***The fact that the black church had to be created.*** The only reason there's a 'black church' is because the white church wanted nothing to do with them.
2. ***Evangelicals' dismissal of the black church.*** Some Christians want to be color blind and criticize the very concept of a black church. Other Christians think blacks are being racists for being in the black church. What they don't realize is that in our history whites kicked them out, and the black church is the only institution blacks have! This is connected to the sin of chattel slavery and what followed.
3. ***Tokenism.*** Think of this as hiring a black pastor to meet

---

[17] Mason, *Woke Church*, 98-112.

some sort of 'quota' and then calling it reconciliation. It's belittling and it happens a lot.

4. *Racial insensitivity in the Academy.* In case you didn't know, the two great giants in church history—Augustine and Athanasius—were blacks from North Africa. Don't forget this.

5. *Evangelical perception of black preachers.* People see T.D. Jakes on television and think that everyone in the black church is like him—as though the black church is made up of people who don't 'really' know the gospel.

6. *That justice is not seen as a primary doctrine.* When you are white and in the majority you are oftentimes blind to matters of justice and oppression, the curse of being removed from the plight of others.

7. *That the Church didn't create and lead the black lives movement.* This is lamentable because the Church should be on the front lines defending those who are victims of injustice. But alas, we just don't care enough, it would seem.

8. *Diminished presence on justice issues.* Black and white churches don't seem to want to talk about these things together, so whites retreat from the conversations and blacks (rightly) get frustrated because of it.

9. *Not effectively equipping the church to know how to engage black ideologies.* Black identity movements are anti-gospel and the Church hasn't been equipped to deal with it.

10. *Giving up on white Christians who want to grow their racial IQ and contribute to healing, resolution, and restitution.* For many black Christians, it can be exhausting trying to get white Christians to see what they see, to hear what they hear, and experience what they experience. Mason doesn't want black Christians to give up because there are many whites who genuinely want to

understand.

These laments are worthy of our consideration, especially as we work towards that grand vision of Revelation 7. However, one of the responses that we *can't* have is the response of saying, "So, I'm supposed to feel guilty about the slavery that I didn't participate in?" This type of retort is common, and it comes from immature people who aren't willing to be humble and listen.

Read what Dr. John Perkins says:

> Some people argue that because slavery occurred more than a century ago, asking people to repent again is beating a dead horse. I understand that, but I also look around and see the legacy that slavery has left among black people— how it has damaged our sense of self-worth so severely and how other forms of bondage have risen up to take its place. We haven't fully exorcised this demon from our national soul. Until we do, our best strategy is to repent. When confession comes out of our mouths, sin is forgiven and room is made for love to come into our hearts. Through love, real change can happen.[18]

I cried the first time I read this, especially the part that said, "...how it has damaged our sense of self-worth so severely." This breaks my heart. It absolutely *crushes* my soul to read something like this. We should be saddened to read such words.

In Daniel 9, Daniel prayed to God and responded to

---

[18] Perkins, *Dream With Me*, 169.

the sins of his people. He *owned them*. He came before the Lord and confessed them as his own. Why? Because Daniel is a member of the covenant. He didn't commit the sins his friends committed, but they became his sins because they were sins against the same God and same covenant. It is not about whether or not you participated in chattel slavery (please hear me!); it's about whether or not you as a Christian are going to be saddened enough to plead with God to bring forgiveness and healing.

I agree with Rushdoony's careful and thoughtful distinction regarding collective guilt and community responsibility. I can't repent for your sin of adultery, and you can't repent for my sin of greed. But together, before the Lord, *we can acknowledge the guilt of the sin, and bear the responsibility to deal with it.*

As a white person in 2020, sure, I can try to simply ignore the history of American chattel slavery. I can try and bury it in the past. However, the problem is, *God doesn't forget history*, nor does he fail to enact justice according to his sovereign will. We need to be vigilant in our *acknowledgement* of the sin, and just as vigilant in *seeing to it that the magistrate deal with the crime.*

So, on one level, you can't repent for someone else's sin. But on another level, you can, as an act of what we might call 'vicarious repentance', confess the sin and strive towards righteousness and justice. This is all done in terms of the covenant.

Humanism as a doctrinal systematic believes that culture is genetics externalized. We call this 'materialistic determinism'. 'Providence by matter' (we might call it), believes that genetic makeup, skin color, and other naturalistic components determines the outcome of societal standing. Some racists have said, and continue to say, that the black person isn't fit for our culture, because their position as a slave is what their genes naturally produce. This is a lamentable sin worthy of stern correction. But people *actually* think these things. They think that whites are the superior race and that everyone else must bow to this imperialism. Kinists today believe it to be a sin to marry across the 'color line'. This, too, is heretical teaching.

The problem with this thinking is simple: *providence comes from the hand of God, not materialism.* Christianity stands in sharp opposition to this thinking, which is rooted in Marxism, because culture is really *religion* externalized. This is not a matter of Darwinian evolution or dialectical materialism. This is a matter of confession: all humans are made in the image of God, and each man and woman possess inherit dignity which is bestowed upon them by God. This is our confession; this is the truth of God's Word. Those who would say that one race is more superior than another will face the Sovereign Lord and be judged accordingly.

When we understand these dynamics properly, we can begin to see things the way God sees things. We can see the beauty in all the nations and the worth and value given to men and women of all tongues and tribes. When we actually and truly grasp this, we can strive towards reconciliation—but only if we truly grasp it.

The reality is, regarding our nation, the sin of slavery is only the beginning. What we see happening now a century later is exactly what Dr. Perkins was talking about. I'll quote him again: "I also look around and see the legacy that slavery has left among black people—*how it has damaged our sense of self-worth so severely and how other forms of bondage have risen up to take its place.*" Anyone whose retort to the suggestion of bearing covenantal responsibility for the sin of slavery by saying, "What, am I supposed to feel guilty?" is a fool who knows not Christ and his covenant law.

The damage done to African Americans is incalculable. Slaves were bought, sold, traded, tortured, raped, beaten, burned, lynched, separated from their family, abused, molested, and treated like dirt. *For several hundred years.*

All so the white man could make a buck. *And the Church justified it.* The beloved Southern theologians like Dabney *justified* it. And after slavery was abolished, the damage still lingered. The concept of police was invented to find runaway slaves. Jim Crow laws followed shortly after. In his book, Dr. Perkins shares some of his stories and personal experience growing up in Mississippi: the white cop who taunted him so as to tempt him to mouth off and get arrested; his brother being shot by a white police officer; and that's just one person! And this was 30-40 years ago!

Today we have the same stuff going on through the vehicle of the drug war. Driving while black is a thing as young men are targeted simply because they are, well, *black*. Someone like Eric Garner is choked to death—murdered on video, mind you—and the cop gets to go home. Philando Castile, Botham Jean, Atatiana Jefferson, and countless other cases… and where is the Church of Jesus Christ? *Ah, yes, they are inside 'just preaching the gospel'.*

And we wonder why there is racial tension in our nation? We wonder why the black sense of self-worth has been scarred and all but completely destroyed? The statist collectivism of white humanists who don't love Jesus has been allowed to run rampant, and it has done nothing but declare war on blacks and other minorities.

So, then, where do we go from here? Well, first, we need to acknowledge it and ask God to forgive us for the sin of American chattel slavery. We need to ask God to use our brokenness over it to move us towards greater reconciliation in the world. We must also acknowledge that the systems in place right now are humanist systems that sustain the injustice. We must also insist on God's just law-word as being the great equalizer that it is. The criminal justice system is broken because the humanists have taken over, and the philosophy of the humanist will inherently mean that minorities and those who do not have the money or means to fight will be oppressed by it. We want righteousness in the public square and that only comes through justice *as defined by God*.

We also need to forge relationships with minorities, not for tokenism, or for the purpose of soothing our guilty conscience, but because the vision of Revelation 7 is our end game, why not do it *now*? Working with black churches, Chinese churches, Spanish churches— you name it—will be a great step. While much more can be said, one thing that we must do is *listen*. Listen to our brothers and sisters and try to understand what they are saying, and in our understanding, let it move us to action.

Americans kidnapped blacks from Africa, ripped apart their families, forced them to work the fields, raped their women, went to war over the right to do so, chased them down with hunting dogs, separated them under the guise of freedom, lynched them, hanged them, dehumanized them, spit on them, and then told them to suck it up, after all, 'That was in the past'.

Some of us are deeply troubled and concerned about the absolute wickedness of this real history and its lingering effects, and the moment one of us speaks up in defense of black men and women everywhere, we're derogatorily labeled a 'Marxist', or 'Social Justice Warrior'. If this what passes for intellectual honesty and integrity in Christian circles, then God help us all. The political tribalism has been and will continue to be (unless we change) a scourge on the Church.

In a manner of speaking: *Church, repent.*

TEN

KINGDOM: THE VISION OF REDEEMED MAN

The angel of the Lord appeared to him and said to him, "The Lord is with you, you mighty warrior."

Judges 6:12

WE COME NOW TO THE LAST CHAPTER OF the book, and we spent nine chapters examining the various ways humanism has wreaked havoc in history and in our time today, and those critiques are ongoing because this is a *war*. We aren't finished with our lamenting and correcting simply because we talked about it once: *this is a war we will continue to fight until humanism is put underneath the feet of King Jesus.* Which means that we must be aware of it and we must be well-versed in it, proving ourselves capable of defeating it; and we must have the vision and conviction as redeemed men, women, and children to actually fight against it.

The war against humanism goes back to the very beginning when Adam and Eve decided to determine for themselves that which is good and evil (Gen. 3:5). When Hebrews talks about maturity, the writer is talking about *theonomy*. The ability to discern between good and evil is a mark of maturity, and that maturity is worked out in how we deal with *autonomy*, self-law, which is the humanist lust. *We deal with autonomy via theonomy*. God's law, in other words, is the only true antidote to man's law. This means that at the core of the theonomic vision is our desire to see God exalted over man, not man over God. This has massive implications, as we will see shortly, but I want to show you from one particular passage how this works itself out.

You're going to want to pause for a moment, grab your Bible, and read Judges 6. To give you a quick contextual reminder, Israel is now in the land, but the enemies of God are not all defeated. Joshua has died and the people decided to stop following YHWH. Because of their obstinance, God brought repeated covenantal judgment. Judges 2:11 says, "Then the Israelites did what was evil in the sight of the LORD and worshiped the Baals." They broke covenant with God and worshiped idols in his place. As a result, God sent judges to deliver them from the hands of those who plundered them (2:16). In other words, we have a theme which dates back to the beginning of time: covenant, sin, redemption, and deliverance. This cycle will repeat several times in the book of Judges.

But how did Israel respond to those like Othniel and Deborah? Judges 2:17 says, "Yet they did not listen even to their judges; for they lusted after other gods and bowed down to them. They soon turned aside from the way in which their ancestors had walked, who had obeyed the commandments of the LORD; they did not follow their example."

Judges 2:18 tells us that God was moved to pity by their groaning because of those who were oppressing Israel. In response, God would anoint a messiah figure to deliver Israel. And thus, the cycle would continue. But what happened after a judge died? Judges 2:19 explains:

> But whenever the judge died, they would relapse and behave worse than their ancestors, following other gods, worshiping them and bowing down to them. They would not drop any of their practices or their stubborn ways.

Covenant reminder, sin, and deliverance; covenant reminder, sin, and deliverance, and so on. Here is where we find Gideon's story, this time focused on the Midianites (who were descendants of Abraham). The reason I chose this passage is because Baalism is the humanist religion which expresses itself in terms of statism, which is the absolute and tyrannical governance and rule of man over other men. This forceful, top-down, humanist rule is wicked, and is partly what Jesus had in mind when he told us not to have authority like the Gentiles who "lord" it over their constituents (Matt. 20:25).

Baalism is statism, and statism is the rotten fruit of the humanist religion. It's fitting that we would look here in Judges to see how best to combat it. So, let's quickly summarize the text here.

In Judges 6:1-10 we get a glimpse as to what was going on. The central sin in Israel was their worship of Baal and because of their apostasy, Israel was on the run. They were oppressed for seven years (v. 1) which is the number of completion. This 'week' is now complete, and the eighth day comes when Gideon is resurrected from the valley of dry bones, given God's Spirit, and will now lead the way as a messiah figure. Note here in verse one that the LORD "gave" Israel into the hands of the Midianites. *The humanists have taken over because God is using them to bring judgment to Israel for their apostasy.* Sound familiar? Due to their idolatry, they were forced into caves, which is a sign of cursedness.

Israel was on the fringes of the land instead of dwelling in the land and now, because of their sin, food had been hard to come by. It was bad enough that the Midianites were oppressing them, the Amalekites were there, too, which tells us just how bad things were (v. 3). Verse six tells us that "Israel was greatly impoverished because of Midian; and the Israelites cried out to the

LORD for help." They cry out to God, but deliverance doesn't just happen right away: God's timing is his prerogative.

First, God sends a prophet to bring judicial charges against Israel. This is an act of grace, though we don't always see it that way. *God's first act of deliverance is a covenantal lawsuit.* Before Christ went to the cross to atone for sinners and be raised for our justification, he brought a covenantal lawsuit to Israel, what we call the Olivet Discourse. Lawsuits are first.

Consequently, repentance is now put on the table for examination: does Israel want to do the hard work of swallowing her pride and turning to God? Or are they just sad enough to be solely concerned about their circumstances? *The prophet explains that it is God who has delivered in the past, and it is God who can deliver right now.* God is able to save, are they willing to repent? God's protection was removed because of *their* sin, will they finally deal with it?

There is interesting language used in verse 10. When God delivers, he has the right to rule over them. *If God is going to save, he is going to rule.* There is no crown without a cross. The lawsuit is now clear: the oppression isn't the problem; their idolatry is the problem. So, what happens next?

As the story goes, God chooses Gideon, and says that he is with him—Immanuel, "God with us." Gideon responds to this promise by faith and prepares a banquet with minimal food and resources (remember that food was a problem and in short supply). Gideon prepares food for a king (bread and wine is such a meal) and the angel of the LORD consumes the food. This ritual is a sign of fellowship and communion with God: The LORD looks at Gideon, literally, "turns" to him (v. 14), which means the relationship and fellowship *is now restored*. Fellowship with God is now the fruit of repentance in Gideon's life.

Another promise comes: God has given Gideon strength to carry out the task before him. What is he to do? *Fight by faith against the humanists who have taken over the hen house.* Gideon is sent to destroy the altar of Baal and the pole of his wife, Asherah. This is a sign of reformation and it starts in his hometown, a principle of localism. Interestingly enough, this altar and pole belonged to his father Joash: *Gideon was raised in a home that worshipped Baal.* Repentance had to start with Gideon, and it had to include his family—this is where Christian reconstruction begins.

In response to this restoration with God, Gideon does the deed at night. When the people wake up the next day, they learn that it was Gideon who had done it, and now they want him dead. But his father Joash thinks that if Baal is a true god, *he'll be able to defend* himself. Baal is given 24 hours to defend his territory. Of course, he can't do so because he's a dumb idol, and consequently, reformation begins to sweep across the land.

A couple quick observations: Gideon replaces his father who was steeped in sin. Think of this as Jesus coming to replace his father, Adam, who had sinned. The other theme present is the younger son replacing the older, which is all throughout the Bible. Jesus is the younger brother who came to upend Adam's failure as the older brother. Gideon was the youngest in the family, in the tribe that was the least of all tribes—how could God use him? This is the mystery of the kingdom of God.

The story here is all about Christian reconstruction. It's about the kingdom of God being the complete and comprehensive vision of redeemed man. It's about God's covenant people doing battle against the idolatry of humanism and statism. If we stop and consider our current situation here in the West, is this not a fitting story?

The Church of Jesus—the ekklesia of God—is currently in a heap of trouble. Many of our key social functions have been commandeered by the humanists. Baalism has run amuck. Universities like Harvard, Yale, and Princeton—founded by Christians and once a bastion of light for the gospel—have been taken over by God-hating statists. Compulsory taxation confronts us at every turn. Humanist licentiousness pervades our media and is paraded in our streets. Unjust policies like the drug war perpetuate the oppression of minorities. Wars of aggression and foreign-military-meddling continues because billions of dollars are poured into the Military Industrial Complex.

From beginning to end, start to finish, top to bottom, our nation refuses to acknowledge the Lordship of Christ and Christianity continues to be pushed to the margins. And *what does the Church do about it?* Repent and have the courage like Gideon and Jesus? No. We do nothing. Not a single thing. By and large, our churches are impotent to do anything anyway because we've theologically castrated ourselves.

Premillennialists have been arguing that it's only going to get worse and they tell us, "Don't worry, Jesus will come and whisk us away."

Amillennialists argue that things are going to get worse, but "Don't worry, you're saved, and you'll get through it," all while perpetuating a two-kingdom theology which says we can't touch the topic of the civil magistrate.

Meanwhile, abortion on demand runs unhindered because we're too busy preaching a truncated gospel inside the four walls of the church building.

Since God is not a liar, we should take him at his

word, and one thing he has told us is that we should pray for his kingdom to come on earth *as it is in heaven*. Which means that this is a prayer he intends to answer. Jesus also intends for the nations to be discipled; remember, God is not a liar. But for the most part, the Church believes God to be a liar because she refuses to believe these words, promises, and expectations. She refuses to believe the truth about Christ reconciling all things whether on earth or in heaven (Colossians 1:15-20). She refuses to believe that Christ has bound up the strongman—the Satan (Mark 3:27). She refuses to believe that the vision for the redeemed man is the kingdom of God here *on earth*.

The Church in America has, for the most part, rejected the Lordship of Christ and embraced the Lordship of the state. And yet, we flat-footedly wonder why things are the way they are? Like Israel, we will whine and complain about the Midianite gay agenda. We'll whine and complain that Canaanites don't say "Merry Christmas" like they used to. We'll whine and complain when a Jebusite Democrat wins, but we're too stupid to see that it's *our* sin, *our* idolatry that is perpetuating the nonsense. Do you see it?

We cry out to the savior-state to rescue us *instead* of King Jesus. We cry out to our church membership to be a salve and balm for our lazy Christian witness. We cry out to everyone and everything but the Lord Jesus Christ and find ourselves up against the ropes and we're bleeding out pretty badly. Farm out your responsibility and you'll reap the devastating sanctions of God.

At what point are we going to wake up and see the covenant lawsuit? At what point are we going to cast aside the idols of Baal? At what point are we going to stop sacrificing our children on the altar of the public school? At what point are we going to tear down the Asherah poles and idols we've erected and turn in repentance towards God so that we can be healed and begin the work of reconstruction? *Now* is the time, and the *Church* of Jesus Christ is where it begins.

The gospel is the royal announcement that a new King has been established and the terms and conditions of his covenant treaty are now available and being enforced. This gospel of the Kingdom is our vision; it's where history is headed. God is always, without exception, the *Creator-Ruler* and man, without exception, is the *ruled creature.* This is ground zero for the war against humanism.

What we must have in our possession is a strategy to seed these ideas into the surrounding culture. We must continue to seed this message in the world using whatever lawful means we have before us.

Friends, we have a lot of work to do and we cannot get distracted, we cannot be lazy, we cannot be selfish. We must be the first in the repentance line because Jesus is Gideon, he's the Valiant Warrior, and we need to follow his rule, starting with you as an individual, with your family, and with the *ekklesia* of God. May God help us.

EPILOGUE

Hot indignation seizes me because of the wicked,
who forsake your law.

Psalm 119:53 (ESV)

THE TWENTY-FIRST CENTURY HAS BEEN
marked by an unchallenged, intractable legal revolution
the founding fathers could have never imagined.
Humanism is no doubt the oldest rival religion to
Christianity. Its power, though, can only grow when
Christians forsake their calling. It is our pietism and
escapism that allows it flourish unabated. When
Christians keep quiet, humanists are emboldened to
speak up.

The greatest ally a humanist can have in order to
advance his statist desire for control and power are
pastors and churches preaching and teaching inevitable
defeat. No one will admit that this is what they're
preaching. And it should be noted, however, that it isn't
always what's said, but what's *not* said. Ignoring cultural
issues and failing to apply biblical law is one aspect of
complicity. Refusing to offer up a biblical worldview
which rivals and rejects the pagan worldview of the

151

humanist is another. Our greatest hindrance, as should be obvious at this point, is ourselves. Our naval-gazing, injustice-ignoring, *selves*.

My hope is for this book to serve as a warning to the humanists and an encouragement to those who are trying to fight. I have talked to so many people across this nation who are sick and tired of being sick and tired. Their pastors won't support their pro-informed consent activities. Their elders will not take a stand against statist intrusion. The world around us is crumbling and the only thing pastors care about is the tithe-money. Don't rock the boat! *I might lose my job.*

Well, consider your boat rocked, fellow pastor. We need courage, and not just the courage to *say* what is right but *do* what is right as well. We need lions in the pulpits and lions on the street. We need churches to stop being inoculated by milk and irrelevant preaching. We need repentance.

I don't yet know how the Lord will use this book, but I pray it will spark an unquenchable fire in our pulpits and churches. Perhaps "hot indignation" may seize us and move us to action. Perhaps.

APPENDIX 1

The following text is a sermon[19] *manuscript* from a message I gave on the topic of vaccines and its relationship to medical tyranny and statism. I believe that this is yet again another issue that falls underneath the "politics of humanism" motif, so I have included it here.

★★★★★★★★★

At first glance it may seem rather strange to hear about a pastor preaching on vaccines, after all, the word doesn't appear in the Bible, the science is settled, and we're supposed to only preach the gospel, right? *Wrong.* There are lots of words that don't appear in the Bible, the science is not settled but obfuscated, and as we'll see today, preaching the gospel means preaching the kingdom of God which is the content and meaning of the gospel.

There are certainly those whose gospel is so far

---

[19] You can watch the sermon here:
https://www.facebook.com/PastorJasonGarwood/videos/86717091372
5925

removed from this earth that it serves no real purpose other than saving souls for heaven, which, incidentally, is a shared presupposition of the gnostic worldview behind statism and Big Pharma. A gospel which is devoid of the kingdom of Christ is a gospel that Jesus did not preach. A gospel which has no real-time historical application for every area of life is a gospel that Jesus did not preach. Our gospel is quite big enough to handle anything and everything in history and life.

When pastors and churchmen balk at the idea of preaching a sermon like this, it is either coming from unbiblical presuppositions (their gospel is impotent), or it is coming from the same erroneous, carnal beliefs of those whom we intend to critique today (their philosophy of ministry is power-oriented and thus it is Gnosticism in practice, just like the vaccine industry).

The reason Christians and pastors should address this topic is because: 1) It is the gospel of the Kingdom of God, and thus the rule and reign of Christ is applicable now, and it should inform our approach to life; 2) Every single area of life is underneath the supreme authority of Jesus Christ, which is what Matthew 28:18 tells us; 3) We are called by the Great Commission to teach nations to obey the commands of Christ, which is another way of saying that those who are obedient to the law of God are to teach the world how to be obedient to the law of God; 4) Using the law-word of God and the authority of Christ, we are to take every thought, philosophy, idea, and systemic injustice captive making it obedient to Christ (2 Cor. 10:5); 5) The Church is called to be light, illuminating nations in what is right and just and true; however, we've become apathetic and lazy, not involved in the things God has called us to; 6) Because of the aforementioned things we can boil the vaccine debate down to this: We are called to the task of the healing of the nations, not the destruction of liberty, human rights, and life. Having said all that, let's consider our three main texts.

Ephesians 5:11 says it clearly: "Do not participate in the unfruitful deeds of darkness, but instead expose them." The apostle Paul tells Christians not to take part in the works of darkness. Why? Because there's a temptation for Christians to do this sort of thing, self-consciously or unconsciously. But there's an assumption here: Christians need to be mature enough to identify the darkness. Which means your senses must be trained. Which means you must understand the law-word of God to such a degree that you are capable of wielding it as you navigate the things in question. Instead of participating in the wickedness, the admonition is to expose the wickedness. We are not to simply ignore the darkness as we retreat to our safe pulpits and churches; we're to reveal it, and uncover it, which activity. Activism is a thoroughly biblical concept.

Romans 3:8 says, "And why not say (as we are slanderously reported and as some claim that we say), "Let us do evil that good may come"? Their condemnation is just." Here Paul address the idea of cheap grace: Christians can do evil and yet God still forgives—as if the gospel can be reduced down to such treachery. If God forgives our sin, they reason, then why not sin some more? Why not do evil so that the good outcome of forgiveness can come? This reasoning is faulty, and Paul goes into further detail on the matter in Romans 6. For now, note that the Bible calls us to condemn this line of thinking when we see the world inflicting harm, or doing evil, because they assume that only good will follow.

Job 14:4 says, "Who can make the clean out of the unclean? No one!" Similar to Paul's logic, Job 14:4 is the principle of trying to take that which God regards as unclean and somehow making it clean. As if we can take aborted fetal DNA, inject it into our muscle, which then moves into the bloodstream, and expect good things to happen. No one can do such a thing, which means the principle must be applied in an ethical manner to the vaccine issue.

In a little while we'll look at Deuteronomy 28, so you can read that before moving on. I'm working with these biblically based principles—and many more—so keep these three texts in mind as we work our way through the issue. So, what about vaccines?

No movement or philosophy or cause in society can make progress and survive for the long haul without an identifiable philosophy of life and religious presupposition being embraced by its shareholders and foisted on its enemies. In other words, it's never if there's a religious commitment of these causes, but which religion is being propagated? It's never if there's a theocracy, but which god is being revered? It's not whether the vaccine industry has an agenda or not, but which agenda are they trying to promote? And what's behind their activity in the world? Any social movement needs philosophical and religious presuppositions in order to advance.

For the Christian, then, we must be able to discern what those things are and bring the gospel into those areas where the gospel will naturally conflict with it. And what we have right now in our nation is a revitalization project known as Moloch worship. My fourth session from the Bible Conference in Zambia covers this, so I'm not going to go into detail now, but just know that Moloch worship is state-worship: the divination of man through the collective means of a centralized nanny-state.

There are plenty of religious and philosophical underpinnings to the vaccine industry, and they are intertwined with the food industry, the rest of the medical industry, lobbyists and politicians, et al.; and of course the common denominator in all of it is statism: the state is god and thereby the final standard and arbiter for all things. When the state creates law, it is final—so they say.

For Christians, this will not suffice; we have a higher law. For those of us who stand on the authority of the Word of God, we believe that God is the one who has power and authority and thus he has providence. We do not believe the state to have these three things. They may have power, but they don't have authority or jurisdiction—not when it conflicts with the authority of King Jesus. And they do not have providence: the ability to control the created order and orchestrate history towards their own means. Only the Triune God of the Bible possess these things.

And guess what? They know this. They *know*. The Bible says that they know God exists and yet they suppress the truth (Rom. 1). But what you need to know is that this suppression is not without a philosophy of life and religious presuppositions. Just because there is suppression doesn't mean there's a vacuum of worldview.

When enemies of the gospel look at the world around them, they see that chaos produced chaos—nothing produced everything—and everything is disordered. Things aren't perfect, so instead of trusting

Christ who is making all things new, they want to escape it. Before they escape it, they want to control it, to sanctify and purify it; they want to be as god, which means they need to attain deity. There are naturalistic, evolutionary presuppositions that fuel Statism, and thus fuel the vaccine industry.

The goal of Christians is perfect humanity, which Christ will accomplish when history is consummated; the goal of the pagan is perfect deity. For the pagan world, sanctification is metaphysical transcendence: using the material world to ascend to the heavens. For the Christian, we want ethical maturity and growth in wisdom and patience and joy. These worldviews are obviously at odds with one another.

And the government-controlled CDC & DHHS are not without these religious commitments, and here is what those commitments are: 1) *Alchemy*; and 2) *Gnosticism*. If man is going to escape living in God's world, he is either going to have to kill himself, or transcend himself. He has to become a new creation; and the way this is done is through power and chemistry; he must abolish time, reach higher consciousness, and escape finitude. He must, quite literally, control the masses through the means of statist interventionism. Government schools, abortion, vaccines—all of it falls under this draconian, alchemist paradigm, including banning unvaccinated children and adults from certain quarters of society.

Regarding alchemy, we're not speaking primarily about ancient magicians in a laboratory trying to make their own fountain of youth. Alchemy, which is what any honest, self-conscious vaccine manufacturer can call himself, is the esoteric science of the religion of Gnosticism. The two go together. Chemical witchcraft under the ostensible guise of "preventing disease" coupled with elitism and secret knowledge (that's Gnosticism) is the statist utopia. Gnosticism does not deal with sin and transgression and moral dysfunction; it can only deal with ignorance, which requires secret knowledge.

However, science should not be a secret endeavor by the elite, government-controlled set of so-called "experts." It must be a publicly disclosed process (where's the double blind placebo controlled test comparing vaccinated vs. unvaccinated, which explains vaccine efficacy?) whereby there is a division of labor, open knowledge with carefully documented data (there should be no government-protected exemptions on disclosures of information and responsibility for its contents), repeatable experimentation (before injecting fetal bovine serum into our bodies, we should probably exhaust the study over and over again (especially given that the 2011 IOM report–IOM is now The National Academy of

Medicine–that the CDC utilizes is filled with a multitude of cries for more data), and lastly, basic consumer law which governs injury to others.

These are all biblical principles scattered throughout the Bible and I'll give you one example: Proverbs 18:17 says, "The first to plead his case seems right, until another comes and examines him." In other words, human life should be of such a value as to exhaust all study, testing, and prospective solutions before administering vaccines. And even then, regardless of the outcome of the science, the individual's right to refuse must remain paramount. (See point #1 of the Nuremberg Code regarding voluntary consent.)

Modern science came because of the Reformation in Europe, not because of the Enlightenment. The only thing the Enlightenment has contributed to science is the attempted confiscation of science for the purposes of humanism and power and control. When men like Freud and Jung came along, they took the presuppositions of the Enlightenment (man is the starting point for everything), married it to alchemy (the science of controlling the material world for the advancement of control and power), and brought it into the realm of psychoanalysis. All of this is connected to the present topic.

Instead of Reformational maturity and ethical progress, the Enlightenment philosopher-kings want transmutation: deification through material control and experimentation. Here is the basic logic: Alchemy needs Gnosticism in order to advance, and both need Statism in order to succeed. And I'm here to tell you that the medical industry, specifically the vaccine industry, has been commandeered by people who hold to these presuppositions. (And yes, there are godly, well-intentioned Christian people involved who are unwitting participants in it.)

But by and large, the CDC has been allowed to concoct their formulas in secret with government backed secrecy and control being the ultimate goal. With regard to alchemy, we're not speaking about methodology only, since alchemy is typically understood to mean uniting the same compounds over and over hoping for a different result. We're talking about the bizarre, secretive, cult-like practices of the vaccine industry which go right along with Gnosticism.

Look no further than what has taken place in California two weeks ago—this will not end there; informed consent, medical/religious exemptions, etc., all of it will be removed by the slow boil of Statism. So that's the worldview behind it; what's the science?

Regarding vaccines specifically, a few things need to be said. The immune system is really two immune systems: Cell-mediated, and humoral. The cell-mediated system, which consists of many different kinds of immune cells and a multi-functional message system (think white blood cells). If we used military terms to describe it, we could say that it is the air, land, and sea attack controlled by different communication systems with the goal of seeking and destroying the "bad" stuff: viruses, bacteria, fungus, toxins, etc. When an unvaccinated child gets chicken pox, the cells are told to go to war, and that's what they do. The end point is white blood cells which either 'eat' the infected cells or disarm the cells with biological mechanisms, but either way, they push them out of the body (which results in rashes or mucus).

Chicken pox and measles, for example, are fought off rather easily by this God-created system, as history has shown. When the frontline cellular armies do their job, they produce symptoms like a fever, which isn't 'sickness', but rather evidence that the body is ridding itself of something that shouldn't be there. In other words, God has created our bodies—down to every last cell—to fight. Our bodies were created good, fully capable of detoxing foreign invasions, and although we are broken because of sin, we need to recognize that we're in the process of restoration, and we must not hinder that process through disobedience and gnostic alchemy, nor should we cavalierly attempt to artificially super-charge such systems with little to no regard for the litany of unintended consequences and side effects.

The humoral system is the part of the immune system that comes along after the fight is over, where the cellular immune system hands over part of the antigen, so that a record of the infection fight is backed up in the body's memory—lymph nodes, in the form of IgG antibodies. If the same antigen should come around in a few years, the body says, "I remember you; you must now leave." These antibodies attach to the remembered antigens and either kill the virus or toxin, or "mark them" so that other cells can come along and finish the job. God knew what he was doing...go figure.

The problem comes in when we introduce the alchemist dream to the process. Medicines like antibiotics (which may have their place), and fever reducing pills like ibuprofen and aspirin, along with vaccines, suppress the cell-mediated response; sure, the fever may go down, but you've just handcuffed your cells from doing their job.

The process is simple: when a child gets measles, the cellular armies chase the invaders in an orderly fashion and destroy them; and the humoral system develops antibodies that remember the virus and are enlisted into the rear-guard immune system army to fight them in the future. If the measles virus comes again, these antibodies destroy it before it can infect other cells; they are the immune system's standing army.

Enter vaccines. Instead of trusting the immune

system process, most vaccines, because they are killed microbes mixed with aluminum, primarily involve the humoral immune system. By design, vaccines trigger the rear-end action of the immune system—the humoral—and quiet down the front line, cell-mediated system. The vaccine turns the core blueprints and functionality for the immune system upside down.

Instead of allowing a child to get chicken pox and fight it the way his body is designed to fight, we inject him with the virus along with other toxins and culture-medium antigens in order to stimulate the humoral antibodies response. In order to accomplish triggering the humoral system without the use of the front line, cell-mediated immune system, adjuvants have to be added to the vaccine: these ostensible "helpers" are irritants that force the humoral immune system to produce antibodies which are supposed to keep out the sickness in question. Vaccines are simply a backdoor 'trick play' on your immune system.

The basic scientific problem with vaccines, then, is the stimulation of antibodies in the humoral immune system, and the suppression of front-line cells in the cell-mediated system. There are two different, though similar, problems with vaccines. One is dysregulation of the immune system because the vaccine is now causing imbalance and mayhem in the system, which may result in a slew of reactions ranging from allergies, autoimmune disorders, chronic illnesses, cognitive disorders, swelling of the brain, seizures, permanent brain injury, and death.

A second problem with vaccines is molecular mimicry where the immune system picks up from the antigen a small genetic sequence which is identical to normal human tissue. This can cause the antibodies to not only attack the antigens in the vaccine, but also begin to track cells in the body which look like the vaccine antigen. Like an angry drunk, the antibodies attack the nervous system, organs, and other vital tissues.

One study done in 2009 in Japan concluded that an overstimulation of the host's immune system leads to autoimmunity in the animals that were tested. In short: vaccines injure both children and adults, because autoimmunity is the result of a misdirected, dysfunctional immune system. And vaccines are *absolutely* the cause.

The question for us is what to think about the CDC schedule and the rise of autism, cancer, and other medical conditions that have grown over the past 50 years. 100 years ago, autism did not exist in medical literature; it was first described in 1943. Then came the era of the vaccine, and suddenly, we're seeing an astronomical increase in autism as the vaccine schedule grows? When hundreds of thousands (if not millions) of parents are giving testimony to the normalcy of their child prior to vaccines, and a subsequent testimony to the severe disruption of that normalcy after receiving vaccines? We're talking 1 in 37 boys with autism. 1 in 37!

And what's inside these vaccines: have you read the inserts? Have you seen the additional ingredients called "excipients?" Let's take aluminum, which is placed in many vaccines as an adjuvant in order to stimulate an antibody reaction. The FDA says that 25 micrograms a day is all that the body can handle. The amount of aluminum given to babies for the Hepatitis B vaccine alone is actually 14 times the maximum allowable dose for an eight-pound baby. When you follow the CDC schedule at 2, 4, and 6-month checkups, infants are given more than 1,000 micrograms! Aluminum alone is connected to various autoimmune diseases, neurological issues, autism, and even MS. Why are we injecting it into our muscles and bloodstream?

Vaccines contain formaldehyde which is used for embalming; it's a carcinogen and can damage the liver and kidneys. Polysorbate 80 is used as a "soap" to make sure the protein antigen doesn't stick to the inside surface of the vial. Its other uses in medicine is to open the blood-brain barrier, so that drugs which would not normally enter the brain, can get in. The question is, does polysorbate result in vaccine ingredients crossing in the brain? If it contains Polysorbate 80, you can bet that the toxins have a greater access to your brain.

How about the flu-vaccine, some of which contains thimerosal, which is a preservative which contains mercury, one of the most toxic substances on the planet? 2 parts per billion is the limit for drinking water; 50,000 (!) parts per billion mercury is in multi-dose flu vaccines that's given to infants and adults.

Bypassing the normal digestive security system, we inject a raft of excipient ingredients into our body tissue, suppress the body's cell-mediated system, and cause dysfunction in the humoral system, all with no scientific understanding of what the immune system does with those diverse ingredients. And we wonder why we 1 in 59 children have autism? And government-backed agencies say that there's no real link between the two, when the studies they cite conclude that at best that it's inconclusive? Is it really that hard to conclude that vaccines contribute to the problem, along with toxic chemicals in our food system? What hath man wrought!

The last thing I'll say regarding the ingredients is the absolute immoral, unethical, and wicked process of injecting animal DNA, and aborted fetal DNA into our bodies. 23 vaccines on the schedule contain the remains of cells, protein, and DNA from aborted babies, the MMR vaccine being at the top of the list. Adenovirus, Polio, DTap/Polio/HiB combo, Hep A, HepA/HepB combo, Rabies, Varicella (Chicken pox), and the shingles vaccines are all on the list. We are abolitionists around here which means we hate the killing of children and we most certainly hate the killing of children in order to sell their parts and participate in the alchemist experiment that is vaccines.

PER-C6, HEK293, IMR-90, WI-38, WI-1 through WI-25, WI 44, MCR-5 are all "human designer cells" but are more accurately called "aborted baby cells." The body is a temple and ought to be honored. And I can think of no other way to desecrate a temple than injecting substances derived from aborted children into our bodies. Christians are by and large not outraged about this aspect to the vaccine industry because the system minimizes the use of aborted baby tissue by saying that it's just a few babies and the ends justify the means. Christians are, by and large not outraged by the sin of abortion. This is because Moloch worship has taken supremacy in our churches; and the Pope, of course, has justified it essentially in the name of Statism.

In Deuteronomy 28 we see the unraveling of the Israelite social order as a result of God's covenant sanctions befalling a disobedient people. The social and economic prosperity given to Israel as a gift would be reversed and taken away so long as Israel pursued idols and refuse to follow YHWH. The land would be cursed, and the ground would yield no crops. Confusion would set it. Verse 22 says, "The LORD will smite you with consumption and with fever and with inflammation." God will send sickness and disease; the same stuff God had done to Egypt in order to rescue Israel (v. 27-29).

Sexual promiscuity will run rampant; thievery and oppression will run about in the streets. Enemies will come and take everything. They will become subservient to another nation (v. 36). Economic collapse coupled with debt incursion will be a new reality. Things will be so bad that mothers will eat their own children, boiling them in their mother's milk. In other words, the thing that's supposed to give life will become a means of death and destruction. God gave Israel the choice to choose life through obedience or suffer the consequences.

God sanctions nations and churches and unfaithful parents who give themselves and their children over to Moloch, be it through abortion or the vaccine industry which leads to injury or even death: a self-inflicted decision. Extraordinary plagues will befall a faithless people and science will not be able to stop it.

There are several final points I'd like to address:

1) The Christian gospel is about moving things from darkness to light. Deceitfulness regarding the alleged pronouncement of safety while concealing the danger, and opting for gnostic (secret) religious presuppositions, is completely antithetical to the Christian gospel. History

is moving from darkness to light, not light to darkness. The CDC & Vaccine manufacturers who are quick to scratch each other's financial back, are actively suppressing information, covering their tracks, and working to control people. And the fact that the National Childhood Vaccine Injury Act of 1986 exists, signed by President Ronald Reagan, proves it.

2) The Bible says that perfect love casts out fear, which means that our gospel gives us the tools to keep us from giving ourselves over to fear in every area of life. God does not give us a spirit of fear. When the media wants to push the "outbreak" button, do not fear. When a doctor wants to warn you about the danger your unvaccinated child may pose to others, don't fear, and remember that some vaccinated children shed and thus can make others sick. Do not fear. When they tell you to fear, you must *not*. When the doctors say, "If you don't do this, your child will die," know that it is a lie, and do not fear. Predestination is a Christian doctrine, but the gnostic religion has its own version, 'let's give you the disease before you get the disease'. Who said I would get it? And who says my body can't deal with it? Who says my God can't deal with it?

3) There is no dignity in death apart from the Christian gospel. The same statist industry that butchers children, that pushes pills and pays off doctors, is the

same industry that wants to control the alleged dangers of disease as well. At best this should give us pause for concern. Whether we live or die, our confession is this: Blessed be the name of the LORD. There is dignity in God's providential hand—even in death. Those who want to do evil assuming that good will be the result have no dignity or honor.

4) Individual liberty wanes the moment we believe the lie that God's law shouldn't be relevant to the discussion. If we will not have the holiness God's law, we will have the tyranny of man's law. And what you're seeing right now is evident of it. Individual liberty, religious exemption, informed consent—these are words that Statists do not understand. We have traded liberty for alleged security, and as someone has said, we'll soon find that we have neither. We have rejected God's law and replaced it with man's law, which means we'll have tyranny: a revocation of religious exemption altogether. Mandated vaccines for children, and you better believe it will come for adults. This is power religion taking control of you. The gospel, and only the gospel, sets you free from all of this.

Lastly… are we insane? You may not participate in Girl Scouts or school or life in this state unless we inject toxic metals, chemicals, animal blood, and aborted fetal DNA into your arm. It's insanity, church. It is confusion. It is fear. It is the unraveling of the

American social order. It's all the things that the gospel combats and restores.

My conclusion? We must stop waiting for the second advent of Christ to accomplish what he has already accomplished in his first advent. The Christian worldview built Western Civilization. It began to crumble, however, the moment we stopped extending those liberties to black slaves. It began to crumble the moment we gave the federal government more and more power. It began to crumble the moment we decided the family unit was dispensable. It began to crumble the moment we decided the Church's job was to keep her mouth shut. It continues to crumble when we allow government bureaucrats to try and run every single area of life through the means of handing our children over to them in matters of health, education, economics, and business. You want my child, Pharaoh? No, you may not.

People who love the gospel of Jesus Christ ought to be suspicious of power and money in the hands of people actively working against King Jesus.

If I get a disease and die, I die. But do we not have the promise of Psalm 91:10, which says, "No evil will befall you, nor will any plague come near your tent." Either way, in my life I have Christ, and in my death, Christ is glorified. Better to die a free man than become a slave of the state with government mandated toxicity

173

coursing through my veins. Jesus is far, far better than that. May the gospel of the Kingdom prevail, and may the Church repent of her apathy, start believing in the promises of God, and start fighting.

We've only scratched the surface: we could go on deconstructing the alleged herd immunity, the lies about the role of vaccinations in eradicating diseases in the past, the whistleblowers who have exposed the lies that are being used to push this program on us, and the twisted claims of vaccination success in poor countries, but we don't have the time. I would refer you to Jordan Wilson's articles at NewCityTimes.com on the matter, as he responded to Joe Carter from the Gospel Coalition.[20]

---

[20] https://newcitytimes.com/news/story/the-gospel-coalition-vaccines-a-response-to-joe-carter

ABOUT THE AUTHOR

Dr. Jason Garwood has spent his career seeking to both understand and apply the Biblical worldview to every single area of life. His aim is to help pastors and churches to be better equipped to engage in the Great Commission by teaching Christians how to find their individual purpose in the Kingdom of God and learn how to identify and respond to cultural idols.

He is currently the teaching pastor at Cross & Crown Church in Northern Virginia:

- Cross & Crown was planted in 2017 with a vision and mission to equip men, women, and children to press the crown rights of King Jesus into every area of life;
- Cross & Crown is a house-church movement seeking to establish other house churches across the world; and
- Cross & Crown is laboring to promote liberty and justice by local activism and involvement in the community.

He is a writer and activist:

- Jason is the author of several books, including *Reconstructing the Heart*, *Have Yourself An Eschatological Christ*, and *The Politics of Humanism*;
- He has written articles for various outlets and blogs at jasongarwood.com; and
- He has preached and lectured internationally on a variety of subjects, exposing the underling errors and problems with anti-biblical worldviews such as: government education, the drug war, the police state, humanist philosophy, and vaccines;
- You can find him at college campuses, high schools, and political meetings seeding the gospel of the Kingdom of Jesus Christ.

Most importantly, Jason is a devoted husband and father:

- He has been married to his wife, Mary, for 13 years;
- They have three children;
- He makes his home in Warrenton, Virginia.